GROWING UP WITH A CITY

By Healy, 1864

PORTRAIT OF MRS. BOWEN AS A LITTLE GIRL, AGED FIVE.

Growing Up With a City

Louise de Koven Bowen

Introduction by Maureen A. Flanagan

UNIVERSITY OF ILLINOIS PRESS
URBANA AND CHICAGO

Manufactured in the United States of America
1 2 3 4 5 C P 5 4 3 2 1

∞ This book is printed on acid-free paper.

Library of Congress Cataloging-in-Publication Data
Bowen, Louise de Koven, b. 1859.
Growing up with a city / by Louise de Koven Bowen ; introduction by
Maureen A. Flanagan.
p. cm.
Originally published: New York : Macmillan, 1926. With new introd.
Includes bibliographical references.
ISBN 0-252-02723-X (cloth : alk. paper)
ISBN 0-252-07044-5 (pbk. : alk. paper)
1. Bowen, Louise de Koven, b. 1859. 2. Women social reformers—
Illinois—Chicago—Biography. 3. Women in charitable work—
Illinois—Chicago—Biography. 4. Charities—Illinois—Chicago.
5. Chicago (Ill.)—Social conditions. I. Title.
HQ1413.B73 2001
303.48'4'092—dc21 2001034732
[B]

TO

ALICE HOLABIRD WOOD

Whose friendship was an inspiration.
Whose loyalty to duty a religion.
And who being dead, yet speaketh
Through the many public interests
To which she gave her life.

CONTENTS

LIST OF ILLUSTRATIONS

INTRODUCTION

Maureen A. Flanagan

Louise Hadduck de Koven Bowen was born in Chicago in 1859 into a privileged and comfortable life. She was the only child of Helen Hadduck and John de Koven, a banker. Her maternal grandfather, Edward Hiram Hadduck, had made a sizable fortune in real estate speculation during Chicago's early years, and Louise inherited part of that fortune. Her husband, Joseph Tilton Bowen, was a highly successful businessman. With her comfortable circumstances, Louise Bowen could have chosen to occupy herself primarily with raising the couple's four children and being a leading member of Chicago society. Instead, even while living the frivolous life of a wealthy young woman, she noticed that other Chicago residents did not have her advantages and set about to make the city a better place. When she finally retired from public activism in 1944, she had spent virtually her entire adult life working for the people of her city. Louise de Koven Bowen's story, however, is not one of noblesse oblige. She literally grew up with her city. Her life and work reveal how, during the turbulent circumstances of the massive urban and industrial change of the time, she came to think of herself as a public citizen and obligated to make Chicago a better place in which to live. She also sought to make the city's government responsible for the welfare of all residents.

Autobiographies generally reveal something of the impulses that motivated their authors to act as they did. Jane Addams, for example, in *Twenty Years at Hull-House,* lovingly describes the influence of her father. Often, individuals who take up public work attribute their actions to the inspiration of a parent or another important adult figure. In *Growing Up with a City,* Bowen says little about her mother, so it is impossible to know what affect Helen Hadduck de Koven might have had on shaping her daughter's ideas and decisions. She never chastises her father, but she does relate several instances in which he discouraged her from acting as anything but a respectable young lady of wealth. He forbade her to play in the yard of neighbor Kate Doggett, informing her that Doggett was a dangerous woman who had radical ideas. Doggett had founded the Fortnightly Club, a woman's literary organization. At the time of his admonition, she was president of the Chicago Woman's Club, whose members were all socially respectable and by today's standards would not be considered radical. But Chicago Woman's Club members demanded that they be allowed to play a public role in investigating and resolving the city's growing problems, something many Chicago men believed to be "unwomanly." When Bowen was sixteen, her father refused to allow her to read an essay she had written at her graduation ceremonies, a public activity he considered "unwomanly." She does mention how early church-related experiences opened her eyes to poverty and the lack of opportunity experienced by many people of the city. Once she immersed herself in public work, however, she rarely again mentions religious inspiration in this book. Nor does she give much account of her personal life after she married. She mentions her husband as being supportive but also tells of his dismay that she was adding another cause to her agenda after she announced at a public meeting that she intended to work for woman suffrage.

With her background and familial pressures, Bowen could easily have chosen to live that respectable, womanly life that her father believed appropriate to her social standing. That she chose otherwise reveals much about her character and indomitable spirit. From the early chapters of this memoir, Bowen reveals herself to be impelled from within to work to change the social conditions of her city. She set out early in life to make a difference in Chicago and pursued that work into her ninth decade.

Bowen's public life and work were so supremely important to her that she focused on that public life rather than on her personal affairs. Her activities are only important in what they can tell readers about Chicago and its growth into a better place. The book's early chapters describing her childhood and young adulthood set this pattern. Chicago was a small but thriving commercial city with a population of just over a hundred thousand when Louise Bowen was born. Some of her earliest memories were of her grandfather's large, comfortable, red-brick house at the corners of Wabash and Monroe streets. Her descriptions of that area reveal a city still young and small enough to have a frontier feel. The house, considered "out of town," was fronted by a dirt road that was almost impassable when wet and muddy and hopelessly rutted when dry. The family kept its own cow, which was driven to pasture down Wabash. Nor were other areas of the city much more sophisticated. Cattle were unloaded at the brand new central railroad terminals and herded through the streets to stockyards outside the city limits.

Bowen's youthful experiences were of a city caught between frontier and urbanity. She tells of how frightened cattle sometimes bolted through the streets and forced her to leap over a fence to avoid being trampled. Yet the visit of a fashionable New York City cousin led her to request that the family coachman be dressed in fancy livery. Her descriptions of the attempt she made when only twelve to bring more style to her family's daily life is at once an amusing personal anecdote and a vivid picture of a young city struggling to wipe the mud from its boots.

In 1886, when Louise de Koven married Joseph Bowen, Chicago had already undergone dramatic change. Skyscrapers were altering the skyline of the city's center. The ten-story Montauk Block building rose over Monroe Street in 1882, just down the way from her grandfather's house. Chicago was also fast becoming the country's premier industrial city. The economic promise of its new mills and factories lured thousands of new settlers, many of them impoverished and foreign-born, every year. The 1890 census counted almost 1.1 million residents. Many Chicagoans rejoiced in the city's massive growth. Some made fantastic fortunes, and many others were able to live comfortable, middle-class lives. What the immigrants found, however, was not so promising. They crowded into squalid tenements without running water or sufficient light and air. The city offered few amenities, fewer public services, and not enough schools.

The industrial economy produced jobs but brought cycles of recession that drove down wages, caused massive unemployment, and deepened poverty. As the disparity between rich and poor widened, workers accused businessmen of mercilessly exploiting them. Radical workers' organizations attracted growing numbers of adherents. In the year Bowen was married, a contentious strike against one of the city's premier companies, the McCormick Reaper Works, led to the Haymarket massacre, in which several people, including one policeman, were killed by a bomb thrown into a crowd at an outdoor demonstration. The subsequent trial, sentencing, and execution of four of the city's prominent anarchists further inflamed the situation. Labor strikes became endemic in the city during the following decades.

By the 1920s, when Bowen wrote this account of her life and work, her grandfather would not have recognized his city. Steel mills, meat-packing companies, railroad car works, farm equipment factories, and other industrial development were now the lifeblood of Chicago's economy. The population numbered almost three million and was distinguished by incredible diversity. A sizable percentage of Chicago residents were foreign-born. Most had come from Europe, although the Mexican population of Chicago also increased from 1,200 to 20,000 during the 1920s. A great migration of African Americans from the South doubled that group's numbers between 1910 and 1920 and then doubled it again across the next decade. Wabash and Monroe streets were now in the heart of the Loop business district. The fashionable twenty-five-story Palmer House Hotel occupied the entire block bounded by Monroe, Wabash, State, and Adams streets. Streets were paved, drained, and well-lit. Automobiles, delivery trucks, and streetcars had replaced horse-drawn carriages. Rather than the de Koven family cow, thousands of office workers and shoppers now whisked along Wabash every day on an elevated electric transit line.

The social conditions of the city that Louise Bowen experienced as she wrote her autobiography were substantially better than those she had encountered as a young woman. In good measure the public work that she and other Chicago women had undertaken since the late 1880s produced the changes. Some of the women, such as Jane Addams and Mary McDowell, are well known because they founded settlement houses, but others are seldom recalled. Their names are unmentioned in most city histories. Louise Bowen's story allows us to enter that woman's world of the late nineteenth and early twentieth centuries and see how women made a difference in Chicago.

Bowen was one woman, but she worked in organizations composed of hundreds and thousands of other women. Her wealth freed her from many daily family obligations that demanded so much of less-privileged women's time. Her position in Chicago society gave her entry into the circles of wealthy philanthropists from whom she could demand contributions to her various causes. Yet she never depended on others to work for her, nor did she accept that giving money was enough to solve Chicago's problems. Because she was privileged, Bowen was able to give and do more than many other Chicago women. She contributed more than $500,000 to the Hull-House settlement, for example. But, to use her own metaphor, she considered herself a third-class train passenger who every day went out and pushed the train uphill because it could not make the grade on its own.[1] She and thousands of Chicago women worked together in female voluntary organizations as third-class passengers. Across the first decades of the twentieth century they pushed uphill, often in the face of ridicule, to change people's lives and build a better city.

What interested Bowen was creating a city that worked not just for the wealthy, or for business, or for Chicagoans who had influence with the mayor, city council, or political leaders. The range of organizations to which she belonged (she served many as president or chair) and the activities in which these organizations engaged demonstrate her interests and her determination to improve the city. Bowen's early concern with the lack of recreation facilities for children, for example, led to a lifelong crusade to provide such services and ensure the facilities were safe and wholesome. In retrospect, she may be criticized for trying to impose her personal, upper-class sensibilities on others. A thread of moral outrage and judgment runs through her work and writings. It is more fair, however, to understand that her concern with vice and protecting young people was a response to the appalling living conditions of many young Chicagoans in the early twentieth century.

The same was true of her work with the juvenile court and the Juvenile Protective Association. Before the organization of the juvenile court, children were arrested for petty offenses and put into jail with adult criminals. Government agencies taken for granted and depended upon now, such as the Department of Children and Family Services, did not exist in the late nineteenth century. Child labor laws were few, and those enacted were often haphazardly enforced. Louise Bowen's description of such conditions paints a vivid picture of a city that allowed its poorest and least powerful residents, children, to be exploited and unprotected by law or government. Her belief that "the forces for good [were] less well organized and active than those that work injury and destruction" (139) was substantially correct. At the turn of the century, few official agencies of municipal government, or even municipal regulations, protected the health, safety, and general welfare of the majority of people in any U.S. city. To read, unjudgingly, Bowen's description of how she worked for juvenile protection allows us to appreciate her efforts to force government to work toward fostering common welfare, although we can accept that she may not always have been correct in thinking that she knew best for young people.

Bowen's passionate belief that all residents had to become involved if a city were to be a better place in which to live, and that they had to work together to achieve that end, led to her decades-long association with Hull-House. Beyond her enormous financial contributions to the settlement house, she served as president of the Hull-House Woman's Club until 1910 and after Addams's death in 1935 was Hull-House's president for nine years. The stated purpose of the Hull-House Woman's Club was to bring together the settlement house's residents, public activists such as Bowen, and the immigrant, ethnic women of the neighborhood "to discuss, investigate and act upon questions of household science, civics, and the advancement of women and the care of children."[2]

The club provided a common meeting ground where women of different classes and ethnic backgrounds could learn from each another and learn to work together. The depth of Bowen's belief in the power of women working together is apparent when she declares in this memoir that "not even in church did I ever get the inspiration or the desire for service, so much as when I was presiding at a meeting of the club" (p. 85). Her experiences also taught her humility. She was chagrined when Addams gently chastised her for thinking that women of different backgrounds and statuses should be grateful for her work with them.

By the second decade of the century, Bowen's work had spread far from Hull-House. In 1910 she helped found the Woman's City Club, an organization dedicated to bringing women together in one central organization to work specifically for the welfare of the city. The club's statement of purpose declared members to be desiring to "assist in arousing an increased sense of social responsibility for the safeguarding of the home, the maintenance of good government, and the ennobling of that larger home of all—the city."[3] Bowen was president of the organization from 1914 to 1915 and again from 1916 to 1924 and was its honorary president from 1924 until she died.

Under Bowen's leadership, the Woman's City Club tried to focus political attention on Chicago's problems. In March 1916 she presided over a meeting attended by three thousand people, many from an array of local women's organizations, at which the club unveiled a "woman's municipal platform" for the city predicated on a "civic ideal which Chicago women hope to attain."[4] The platform demanded more and better schools and housing, reformed health and sanitation standards across the city, more recreation facilities, the same concentration on crime prevention as on law enforcement, and protection of women workers' right to strike.

When Bowen recounts this mass meeting and its aftermath a decade later, she is optimistic that women's efforts were bringing about important social changes in the city. That point of view characterizes the entire memoir and reflects her understanding that change requires years of steady, patient work. She tried always to celebrate what had been accomplished rather than dwell on what had failed. She and other women often failed to achieve much of what they wanted; few of the proposals of the woman's municipal platform, for example, were adopted as public policy. Despite that discouraging lack of response, however, Bowen and other Chicago women kept working, third-class passengers who knew they had a long haul in front of them. As the city prepared to contribute to the war effort with the U.S. entry into World War I, Bowen describes how women sought to turn that tragic circumstance to their advantage, working to convince city leaders that attention to social welfare, especially better child care, would help the war effort and guarantee a brighter future for Chicago.

The woman's municipal platform and the local efforts during World War I are just two of many forgotten pieces of Chicago's history that Bowen's account brings to light. Her political experiences also provide a firsthand account of how the parties treated civic-minded women when they were able to vote. Bowen actively supported woman suffrage and was serving as president of the Chicago Equal Suffrage Association when in 1913 the Illinois legislature gave the women of the state the vote in local and federal elections. She immediately took up the task of convincing women to register and vote in Chicago's spring 1914 municipal elections. She was certain that women's votes would make a great difference in reforming the city and its government and that women would vote independently. As she was quoted in the *Chicago Tribune,* "I do not think the husband will influence the wife's vote in municipal affairs."[5]

Women may have voted independently, but most men still considered them second-class citizens, as Bowen demonstrates with anecdotes of the early 1920s. In 1912 she had supported the Progressive Party led by Theodore Roosevelt. After that party's virtual demise, however, she viewed the Republican Party as the best hope for securing what she wanted from government. Yet she encountered a series of obstacles that created still another uphill battle. She describes how the men who controlled the party wanted only women who "were to do the men's bidding" (pp. 207–8). Chicago Republicans condescendingly rebuffed almost every effort she and other Republican women made to be treated as equal party members. Although she does not dwell on the experience, when Bowen briefly flirted with the idea of running for mayor in 1923 she and other women were publicly ridiculed for thinking that a woman might be capable of holding that office. One newspaper account observed that a woman could not be mayor because "ladies are not always guided by sober judgment, but rather by their emotions and impulses."[6] Her mild account of the episode in her memoir exemplifies sober judgment. She attacks neither those who publicly denigrated her nor those among her male allies in reform who failed to support her. She does, however, later describe her amusement at the panic her possible mayoral bid caused, even among her closest male friends and allies.[7] Her response to the situation is yet another example of optimism in the face of adversity. Rather than complain about her treatment, she asserts that the gambit resulted in the parties choosing good men to run for mayor.

A contemporary reader could justifiably note Bowen's absence of attention to matters of race. The great northward migration of African Americans began during World War I, but she mentions neither the impact of the movement on Chicago nor the tragic 1919 racial riot in the city. In addition, she does not discuss the work of African American women's organizations in Chicago. There is evidence in other sources, however, of some of her responses to the race issue. In 1913 she published the results of an investigation into the social conditions of the city's African American community and decried the lack of opportunity, especially for African American young people. In 1917 she rejected a request that she, as president of the Woman's City Club, denounce the employment of a black physician at the Municipal Tuberculosis Sanitarium, saying that the doctor had every right to employment there. Two years later, as a stockholder in the Chicago Telephone Company, she wrote to its president, urging him to hire African American women as telephone exchange operators. In addition, she worked with African American women against racial discrimination in housing and juvenile justice as well as in the suffrage movement.[8] Perhaps her lack of forthrightness on the issue of race relations is in keeping with the tone of the rest of the autobiography, which accentuates positive achievements and conciliation rather than differences. The rise of the urban Ku Klux Klan, which drew adherents in Chicago, might have made her hesitate to include anything that would make her book a target of racists and thereby detract from her broader message.

Growing Up with a City, in fact, generated much national interest. It was reviewed in newspapers throughout the country as well as in national magazines such as the *New Republic* shortly after it was published. It received the kind of response Bowen was surely seeking. Review after review emphasized how her book was more a social document than a personal record and praised it for its wit, information, and nonjudgmental tone. The *New Republic* singled out its last chapter for showing how the "unfailing public spirit and energy" of Chicago women were improving municipal conditions. One anonymous Chicago resident wrote to tell Bowen that although he did not know whether she had intended to inspire others to work for the city, reading the book had given him a "glow of renewed purpose." A professor of economics asked her permission to reprint the chapter on the Juvenile Protective Association in an anthology of vocational readings that he was preparing for eighth-grade and early high school students.[9]

As Bowen closed her memoir, she looked with pride on a city much changed. It was, she believed, a city much changed for the better from the one that had prompted her to undertake her public work. As she wrote in mid-decade, she was surely optimistic about the city's future. Her mayoral gambit in 1923 helped convince Republican Party leaders to replace their incumbent mayor William Hale Thompson with a more reform-minded candidate. The Republican candidate, Arthur Lueder, had lost, but Bowen and other civic-minded women believed the new Democratic mayor, William Dever, to be an honest politician who would continue to bring reforms to the city. When Thompson regained the mayor's office in 1927 she was so dismayed that four years later she joined the Women's Independent Committee for Anton Cermak, the Democratic nominee. Cermak, she observed, had "made such a good record for himself in the management of the various charitable institutions of Cook County" that she was confident that his election would produce "lasting benefit to the city."[10]

Whatever obstacles she encountered in her fight to make Chicago a better place for all its people, Louise Bowen never lost her sense of outrage over injustice and inequality of opportunity—or her optimism that reforms could be accomplished if all people worked together. A letter she sent to the Woman's City Club in 1952, when she was too ill and frail to address that group in person, is proof that at ninety-three she still adhered to principles that had always guided her. Addressing her "Beloved Woman's City Club," Bowen declared that she longed "once again, to stand before you and speak out in ringing tones a denunciation of present day politics." Casting her eye on the frightening international scene of the early 1950s, she considered the problem in the terms of an earlier time. Nations, she explained, could not live in peace "unless the individuals within the nations learn to live peaceable side by side, family with family, and within each family."[11]

In many ways Louise Bowen was not unique among women of her generation. Millions of urban women organized to challenge the harsh realities of urban industrial life in the United States at the end of the nineteenth century and simultaneously demanded that women be given a public space and voice. Far too often, however, their voices and actions have been ignored in our telling of history. What Bowen does provide is a rare portrait of the city of Chicago from a woman's perspective. *Growing Up with a City* shares the optimism of the urban activism of women early in the twentieth century that all people could learn to live together and create a better society.

NOTES

1. The metaphor is from a speech de Koven gave in 1902 at the anniversary of the founding of the Hull-House Woman's Club. Louise de Koven Bowen, *Speeches, Addresses and Letters of Louise de Koven Bowen, Reflecting Social Movements in Chicago* (Ann Arbor: Edwards Brothers, 1937), 1:61.

2. *Hull-House Bulletin* (1902–3).

3. Woman's City Club of Chicago, *Bulletin* (July 1911). See also Maureen A. Flanagan, "Gender and Urban Political Reform: The

City Club and the Woman's City Club of Chicago in the Progressive Era," *American Historical Review* 95 (Oct. 1990): 1032–50.

4. "Report of Proceedings: Mass Meeting of Women to Protest against the Spoils System and Adopt a Woman's Municipal Platform," March 18, 1916, folder 1, Woman's City Club of Chicago Manuscript Collection, Chicago Historical Society.

5. *Chicago Tribune,* Feb. 1, 1914.

6. *Chicago Tribune,* Dec. 19, 1922.

7. Sharon Alter, "A Woman for Mayor?" *Chicago History* 15 (Autumn 1986): 53–68.

8. Louise de Koven Bowen, *The Colored People of Chicago: An Investigation Made for the Juvenile Protective Association, by A. P. Drucker, Sophia Boaz, A. L. Harris, and Miriam Schaffner* (Chicago: Rogers and Hall, 1913); *Chicago Examiner,* Jan. 30, 1917; Louise de Koven Bowen to B. E. Sunny, president, Chicago Telephone Company, 1919, in Bowen, *Speeches, Addresses and Letters,* 503; Anne Knupfer, *Toward a Tenderer Humanity and a Nobler Womanhood: African American Women's Clubs in Turn-of-the-Century Chicago* (New York: New York University Press, 1996), 46.

9. Bowen collected the reviews in four volumes of scrapbooks that are now in the Chicago Historical Society.

10. *Chicago Tribune,* April 5, 1931, clipping in Louise de Koven Scrapbooks, vol. 3, Chicago Historical Society.

11. A copy of this letter, dated January 19, 1952, is in "Louise de Koven Speeches" folder, box 3, Nancy Cox–McCormick Cushman Manuscript Collection, Sophie Smith Collection, Smith College Library.

PREFACE

In writing the following record I feel as though I had dug up my whole life. raked it over thoroughly and thrown the result on blank pages.

It has been very difficult to look back through the years and put the various organizations with which I have been associated in any logical sequence, as I was always connected with several at the same time.

I do not, of course, pretend in any way to have brought about the social changes which are recorded here; everything that has been accomplished has been through the mutual efforts of a remarkable group of women who have been my contemporaries in Chicago.

In my hospital work, in the United Charities, at Hull-House, in the Woman's City Club, all through the dark days of the war and in my first stumbling efforts in politics, these women have been a constant source of inspiration and assistance.

My thanks are also due to the many friends who have listened so often and so sympathetically to the stories contained in this book, and who have encouraged me to put them into print. To all these friends and to the women who have been identified with me in these various undertakings, I am deeply indebted and I acknowledge with gratitude their support and encouragement.

LOUISE DE KOVEN BOWEN.

GROWING UP WITH A CITY

GROWING UP WITH A CITY

CHAPTER I

A GRANDCHILD IN EARLY CHICAGO

Because my grandfather lived in Fort Dearborn and my mother was born within its palisades, I naturally heard, from my earliest childhood, many stories of that valiant band of settlers, traders and soldiers who made their home in what was then a wilderness and who endured hardships and braved dangers in order that they might establish a settlement between the East and the Mississippi River.

My early imagination was caught by the stories of Mrs. La Compt, a most remarkable woman who came to Chicago during the latter part of the 18th century; she was married three times and lived until she was 109 years of age! Mrs. La Compt was a woman of great mentality and an extraordinary constitution; she was also possessed of remarkable courage. She had always been good friends with the Indians, she spoke their language and developed a remarkable influence over the Pottawatomies. She would often be awakened in the dead of night by an Indian friend who would tell her that the Indians were contemplating an attack on the white people. Instead of seeking her own safety, she would always set out alone to meet the war party and never failed to avert bloodshed. Sometimes the settlers would arm themselves and await the attack and after two or three days they would see the hostile Indians approach with Mrs. La Compt at their head, their hostile war paint changed to sombre black, to show their sorrow for having entertained evil designs against her friends. This all sounds too good to be true, but I believed it then and I have properly verified it since.

I was told that in 1803 troops from Detroit, under Captain Whistler, were ordered to Chicago. When they reached their destination they found a few traders and friendly Indians, and they determined to settle near the mouth of the river, which they found about ninety feet across, eighteen feet deep, and surrounded by low banks covered with bushes. There was then a sand bar at the mouth of the river over which the troops walked dry shod. A fort was built as soon as possible. The Indians seemed friendly but bothered the soldiers greatly by their thieving. Many traders settled around the Fort and exchanged liquor for furs, so that rum played a big part in the building of the Fort just as it did later when it was demolished.

All early Chicagoans know that Fort Dearborn was maintained in Chicago for nine years. It was a tedious life for the soldiers, with little excitement except an occasional scare from the Indians and the arrival of some vessel bringing supplies to the little group of soldiers and traders in the settlement. There was an abundance of game; deer were frequently seen swimming in the river and wolves were often heard howling at night.

The stories of the Indians were scarcely less exciting than those I sometimes heard of the soldiers. The personnel of the army at this time was not very high, drunkenness was common and the usual punishment was a certain number of lashes. Sometimes the culprit was forced to run the gauntlet between two rows of soldiers, both ranks striking at the same time. Sometimes he had his head shaved, a bottle tied around his neck and was drummed out of the settlement to the tune of the Rogue's March.

In 1810, years before my grandfather came to Illinois, Nathan Heald succeeded Whistler at Fort Dearborn; he married in Louisville and brought his wife to the Fort on horseback, accompanied by her black slave girl who was the first slave owned in Chicago. When the war of 1812 with the British was at its height, hostile bands of Indians were so numerous that Captain Heald received orders to evacuate Fort Dearborn and go to Detroit. These orders he was loth to obey as the Fort was well provisioned and he felt it could hold out a long time, while if it was abandoned its inmates would not have a chance of reaching a place of safety, as the country was filled with Indians, many of whom were crazy from liquor sold them by the white traders.

Captain Heald, however, was a soldier and trained to obey orders, so he had no choice; the government sent him thirty Indian warriors to help the little garrison, these men being under the command of Captain William Wells, a famous scout for whom our Wells Street is named.

Captain Heald ordered that all liquor in the Fort should be destroyed and this is said to have so infuriated the Indians that it was one of the reasons for the massacre the following day. All preparations being now completed for the evacuation of the Fort, there issued forth the most forlorn little procession Michigan Avenue has perhaps ever seen. First came the Commander and some of the friendly Indians with their scout leader, then the militia, Captain Heald's wife and the wife of the Lieutenant, on horseback; then the women and children in wagons surrounded by the soldiers, while friendly Indians guarded the rear. The party went south on Michigan Avenue, which was then just a sandy beach, with sand dunes on the western side, the lake coming up to the avenue, until they reached what is now known as Eighteenth Street. Then Captain Wells, who had gone ahead, was seen coming back, waving his hat in the direction of the west, and from behind sand dunes could be seen the heads of

Indians, who swooped down on the little party. The friendly Indians immediately deserted, the children and some of the women were killed at once; Captain Wells fought so bravely that after his death the Indians cut out his heart and ate it, which was the greatest compliment they could pay him. Captain Heald finally surrendered on condition that the prisoners should be spared. Many of these prisoners, however, were tortured and some were burned at the stake; nine men were taken prisoners who were kept as servants and two years later they were sold to some traders and liberated. One of these men was named Joseph Bowen; he was, however, not related to my husband.

The story of one of the men who survived the massacre is interesting. His name was David Kennison; after the massacre his skull was crushed by a falling tree, he had a bad fall later and broke his collar bone and two ribs, the discharge of a faulty cannon broke both his legs, a horse kicked him in the face and smashed in his forehead. Nevertheless he survived all these injuries, was married four times and had twenty-two children; the last two years of his life he entered a museum, as he felt his many adventures made him an object of interest, and his pension was not enough for him to live on. He died in 1852 at the age of 115 years, in full possession of all his faculties. He was buried in Lincoln Park and, when most of the bodies buried there were moved, his was not disturbed, and in 1905 a monument was erected over his grave by some patriotic societies.

In 1815 another expedition was sent to re-establish Fort Dearborn, and it was occupied on and off until 1832, when it again housed a garrison. This was the time of the Black Hawk War and the Fort was crowded with settlers who had taken refuge there, something like two hundred people being housed under its hospitable roof. My grandfather, Edward H. Hadduck, came to Chicago about 1835. He was in charge of $200,000.00 which he brought in a prairie schooner wagon from Detroit to Chicago. This money was to be used to pay the Indians for certain obligations which the government had incurred. When my grandfather reached Chicago he saw so many possibilities for a young man that he immediately returned to Ohio, married my grandmother and brought her to Chicago. They were obliged to take refuge in the Fort and I have often heard my grandmother tell of the trials of living in the same room with fifty other people, and how difficult it was to get water and how she had to sneak out of the Fort down to the river, to avoid the Indians of whom she was very much afraid.

Help finally came from the East but the garrison had hardly settled down before cholera broke out and many people died of it. From this time, Chicago forged steadily ahead. Her position at the foot of Lake Michigan on the great highway of

OLD FORT DEARBORN IN 1856.

trade secured her commercial advantages which no other city could rival.

I became so familiar with the stories of these early days that it is most difficult to disentangle them from my actual experiences, but my earliest recollections are clustered around an old fashioned red brick house which belonged to my grandfather and which was set far back from the road on the corner of Wabash Avenue and Monroe Street. There were shade trees in front of the house and a broad strip of green sward before the roadway was reached. This road was made of good black prairie soil. When it was muddy it was almost impassable and when it was dry there were huge ruts which shook up everyone who drove over them. At one time there was a hole in the road opposite our front door and two boards were stuck in it on one of which was roughly scrawled, "No bottom here; good road to China."

When my grandfather built this new house and moved from his Lake Street residence out to it, the neighbors all regretted that he and my grandmother were to live so far out of town, where it would be difficult to meet together in the evenings for the parties they so often enjoyed.

The house itself was big and roomy. The front door, on Wabash Avenue, was never opened except twice a day—once when my grandfather went to his mill in the morning and once when he returned at night, he having a partiality for that door and refusing to use the side door, which stood unlatched during the day for the use of the other members of the family.

I always met my grandfather when he came home at night. He was an interesting figure, wearing black broadcloth clothes with a high collar, an old fashioned black stock, and, alas, a large diamond solitaire in his shirt front. His high hat was always shiny as well as his right coat sleeve, which served instead of a hat brush. When he came home at night he was all covered with white dust from his mill and I used to get a brush to help him leave this dust on the doormat rather than take it into the immaculate hall. I can see him now, as he would put his head in the door and call to me; then, as I came running down the stairs he would take off his tall hat, which was full of papers of all descriptions, leases, deeds, mortgages, bank notes, even the morning paper and usually something he had brought home for me. I used to say to him: "Grandfather, how do you manage to get your hat off when you see a lady on the street?" He would chuckle, and reply, "Oh, I just shake the brim of it a little." When I said, "Why don't you carry your money in your pocket?" he would answer, "My dear, your grandmother does not like to see me with my pockets bulging."

On one occasion my grandfather climbed up a ladder in order to look at a new building belonging to him which was in process of erection. He lost his balance and fell from the second story to the ground. When he was picked up unconscious, the tall hat, full of papers, was crushed down over his head and after it was almost pried off of him he was found to be unhurt except for a slight cut. The tall hat had saved his life, and in commenting on it afterwards he said to me quizzically, "My dear, always wear a stiff hat when you climb a ladder."

On one occasion he came back from town and taking off his tall hat said, "I sold the corner of Washington Street and Wabash Avenue" (where Marshall Field & Company now stands) "for a good sum and I am going to divide it between you and your mother." With that he pulled out bank notes and checks and made a fair division. This was the first money I ever had and it gave me an annual income which I was allowed to spend as I chose.

To the right of the front hall in the red brick house was a huge parlor. It was always kept shut except on rare occasions, when we had a party. It had huge mirrors at either end and the chairs were shrouded in sheets. The carpet was a wonderful study in green and white, representing an African jungle where, underneath obese bananas, succulent pineapples and waving palms, little lambs played with snakes and lady-like lions sat down with the lambs.

A little marble-top table stood in the middle of

the room, on which reposed the family Bible and on Sundays, when I was good, I was shown the awful pictures in this holy book and told of the horrible fate awaiting those who wandered from the straight path. There were also what-nots and etageres about the room, filled with ugly bric-a-brac of every description, and on the mantel, between two candlesticks, stood a glass covered monstrosity of wax flowers. I remember one day going into this room on tip-toe to see what it really looked like. I suddenly saw another figure advancing toward me. I gave a scream and rushed for the door, upsetting on the way a statuette of the Prodigal Son, and flung myself into the arms of a small cousin who had come to spend the day with me. The result of this encounter was that my cousin's front teeth found my forehead very hard, the teeth were picked up from the carpet and I was borne bleeding from the room, only to be reproved later for playing in the front parlor.

In those days I was a pale, anaemic-looking little child, a fit subject for a nutrition class. I was always around with a book called "Reading without Tears" under my arm, which belied its title for I wept copiously over it every day. I quote a few choice selections culled from this book. Some of the incidents set forth may have been common in child-life in the early days, but I do not remember having any of the adventures recorded, such as:

"I met a cat in a bog."
"A wig is on a hog."
"There is a pen in a bog."
"I have a red bed."
"I saw a wet hen."
"I spy a blue cat."
"I fed ten men in a den," etc.

As I almost always had an earache or a sore throat, I usually had a hot onion tied over one ear, or else a piece of raw salt pork around my throat, as these, pork and vegetable products were considered good for these respective ailments. I hated myself because I smelt of onions and meat and I seriously considered suicide in the cistern which supplied the house. Possibly one reason for my poor health was that one of my principal occupations was poking around in a dark cellar where, on a high shelf, were crock after crock of different kinds of pickles, all of which I sampled every day.

I used to play in front of the house a great deal, because the open air was thought to be good for me. Across Monroe Street was an old garden belonging to Mr. Eli B. Williams. It had all kinds of fruit in it, and, though I was never invited to pick this fruit, there were occasions when I visited the garden uninvited and partook lavishly of gooseberries. I remember one occasion in particular when I almost stripped the gooseberry bushes and immediately afterward drank nearly a pint of cream which I stole from our cellar. The result was so disastrous that I never visited the garden again.

We kept a cow and one of my chief amusements was helping the hired man drive this cow, every morning, up Wabash Avenue to a vacant lot on Adams Street, where the cow ate heartily most of the day, coming home only in time to be milked. I can well remember, when this lot was afterwards built up, that my grandmother complained bitterly that the city was making no provision for the feeding of the cows of its citizens and she said, "What are we to do for milk if our cows cannot get fresh food?"

Adams Street was then so far out of town that one adventurous pioneer who had built his house on that street had it face north so that he could look toward the town, see the lights at night and not feel lonely.

In these early days the cattle for the Stock Yards were unloaded at the Randolph Street Station of the Illinois Central Railroad and were often driven through the streets to the Yards. Michigan Avenue was not much more than a sandy beach, and as Wabash Avenue was a harder and better roadway, the cattle were frequently driven down this avenue. Sometimes the steers would become frightened and would rush from one side of the street to the other, coming up onto the sidewalk and imperiling the passers-by. Many a day I have quickly climbed over the low iron fence around my grandfather's yard in order to get away from the frightened beasts. Indeed, the streets were not much safer sixty years ago than they are today, although the dangers were slightly different.

Walking along Wabash Avenue one morning, I heard a great outcry and was suddenly seized by a man who, carrying me in his arms, rushed up the steps of a house, ran into the vestibule and shut the outside door. I immediately began to kick and scream until he said, "Be quiet, you little fool! There is a mad dog out there!" And sure enough, a large mad dog, foaming at the mouth, ran past. I remember another innocent looking worn-out dog who took refuge on our front porch and, for some reason, was supposed to be mad. There was an old saying at that time to the effect that if a dog did not like cold water it was surely mad. We did not dare to open the door to throw the water but my mother and I pulled the window down from the top, filled a dishpan full of cold water, and my mother, mounting a stepladder, dumped the water unceremoniously on the head of the unoffending dog. He naturally snarled his disapprobation at this Niagara and fled to another part of the porch, while the whole family solemnly asserted that the dog was surely mad because it did not like water. I was dispatched out the back door to the nearest police station to get an officer; he came, and perpetrated what remains in my mind to this day as a brutal, cold-blooded murder.

Another time, while walking with a child on Congress Street, just opposite the present Auditorium Hotel, an infuriated bull came rushing up the street. I saw him in time and managed to scramble over the fence, but my companion was hastily tossed into the yard belonging to Mrs. L. Z. Leiter, who took us in and comforted us, our feelings and our clothes being somewhat torn by the encounter.

We were country folks in those days and often went for all day picnics to the old Gage Farm on Michigan Avenue near Sixteenth Street. It was a day's outing to get down there and back and it took a long time to drive through the sand on Michigan Avenue. We were often bothered by what we called "green heads," large black flies with green heads which drove the horses and even people nearly wild. I remember our horse wore a black rubber net which shook as he moved and I even covered my head with the lap robe to keep from being stung by the green heads. As we slowly drove our horse and buggy my grandmother would tell me stories of the early days in Chicago when she lived in the Fort and used to ferry herself across the Chicago River on a little flat boat which was propelled by the passenger pulling a rope stretched across the river. She would tell me how she used to go to the North Side to pick blueberries; how oftentimes she would hear an Indian coming and would crouch down beside the bushes until he had passed. Then there were thrilling tales of Indian massacres and of her experiences of being shut up in the Fort while the Indians bombarded the place, shooting flaming arrows into the Fort and often attempting to set it on fire, and how happy the beleaguered were when the scout, who had been sent out to get help, returned with some soldiers, and the Indians were dispersed.

She told me of her first house on Michigan Avenue near South Water Street; of how convenient it was, that she actually had a sink and the water ran away in it. The lake wasn't far off and all she had to do to get water was just to take two pails across the road and dip water out of the lake and bring it up to the house; she said "It was like playing at housekeeping to have everything made so easy!"

She would point out to me, as we drove around in our buggy, the prairie schooner wagons, which were often seen on our streets, and she would tell how my grandfather had come for her to Ohio in one of these wagons, and brought her all the way to Chicago; of what a lovely drive it was, although as they drove she sat with a loaded rifle across her knees. She told me of paying fashionable calls when she lived on Lake Street. The mud at that time was very deep, so that at times it was almost impossible to cross the street. When she first went there to live she would borrow a neighbor's ox-cart, which was thoroughly scrubbed and a plank put across the cart; it would then be backed up to the door and my grandmother and her friend, attired in clean calico dresses, mounted the ox-cart, took their seats on the plank and were conveyed to the various houses where they were going to call.

When I was five years old we moved into a little house on Michigan Avenue just opposite Park Row. It was, of course, way out of town and very far for me to go to school because Dearborn Seminary, which I attended, was where Marshall Field's Wabash Avenue store is now located, so I was sent to an old dame's school, half a block away from home, where I endured a perfect purgatory. My seatmate, for we sat at double or intimate desks, had I suppose, epilepsy, and at least several times a week I would raise a shaking arm, and say, "Please, teacher, Belle is having a fit." Poor Belle would then be almost pried off of me, as she invariably clutched me around the neck and refused to release me. When I went to this school it was at a time when every girl wanted to have curly hair and if nature had not so endowed her, she purchased her "fringe," as we called it, by the yard. It was black or brown or red as the occasion required, and this fringe was sewed into each girl's hat. I can remember seeing rows of these hats, with the hair sewed in, hanging on the racks of the little coat room.

Dearborn Seminary was later moved to Twenty-second Street and Wabash Avenue and I then attended this school, driving there with my pony in a little low phaeton and putting the trap into a nearby stable while I was at school. Later on, when I graduated from this seat of learning in my sixteenth year, fully versed in all the isms, our graduating exercises were held in a large church. The twelve girls who stood highest in the class, attired in white muslin dresses with blue sashes, read their graduating compositions on the platform to a large and appreciative audience of parents, admirers and friends. I had composed a very elegant and artistic essay, rather foreign to my character. It was entitled:

> "Silently sat the artist alone,
> Carving a Christ from an ivory bone."

The essay began as follows:

"The artist is king; he reigns over a mighty realm. His dominion is not bounded by earth or the stars. In his chariot of fancy, drawn by winged steeds, he travels through space, through cloud and sunshine; through light and darkness, until his object is attained; floods cannot drown—fires cannot burn his possessions. His title deeds date from Adam. When God breathed into him the breath of life, then the grant was given to mortal man, in dreams to see things invisible; in dreams to move and breathe and live a life which touches the Divine. All men are not given thus to live."

Having thus soared around in the clouds and held communion with a few of the planets, I descended to earth, and, as I remember, the remainder of my essay was about the working man and his difficulties. But I felt in my youthful enthusiasm, that I must deal with a few things of the spirit, and therefore soared like a small skyrocket prematurely set off. I considered the essay a work of art, but unfortunately my father would not allow me to be so unwomanly as to appear in a crowded church and take part in any graduating exercises; I was therefore not allowed to read my essay, but sat at the foot of the platform with those who stood lowest in the class, and listened to my more fortunate friends in their oratorical flights. It was no consolation that morning to have been allowed to read my essay before the pupils of the school, for I felt they were not old enough to appreciate intelligently my flight into the realms of fancy.

It has often been my bad fortune to have to collect money for charitable purposes here in Chicago, but I do not think I shall ever forget my first experience in begging. A little girl walking down Michigan Avenue was crushed against a lamppost by a runaway horse and her arm broken. I was very much interested in the affair and finding there was no money to pay the doctors, I started to raise fifty dollars for that purpose. Going up and down Michigan Avenue I inquired at each house for the lady of the house (I knew almost all of them and they knew my family). I would then ask for fifty cents for the child and in almost all cases it was given to me. I shall never forget, however, the hurt to my pride when one of the richest of Chicago women, living in what was then a marble palace, not only refused to give me the fifty cents, but upbraided me for begging at her door, literally driving me down her steps with rough words and rougher gestures. Even the fact that I was able to collect in all $57.50 never made up to me for this, my first rebuff.

Although I had graduated from Dearborn Seminary, I did not feel that my education was finished and for the next two years I prescribed for myself a careful course of study which consisted in using the Cyclopedia, looking through the index, finding the subjects which interested me and studying them conscientiously. It could not be said that this study was along any one line; it certainly gave me a broad outlook. About this time my education was also being completed in the arts and in fine handiwork. I was made to practice one hour a day at the piano and after several years of study was able to play "Comin' Thru the Rye" and "Nearer My God to Thee." I also took lessons in making wax flowers in which I became quite proficient. My handiwork, when completed, consisted of large bouquets of roses, japonicas, camelias and violets. These were treasured by my parents and a glass case put over each effort, which was then placed on the etagere. My fancy work, when we were *en famille,* always consisted of hemming sheets and wash cloths. By the time I made my entry into society I was ignorant in everything and accomplished in nothing.

There were many evidences of culture in Chicago at this time. New York was regarded as the hub of the universe and whenever our family went there we always brought home something highly recommended to us. I remember that on one visit there when bronzes were in style, we purchased a large bronze Pocahontas, too big for the little canoe in which she was seated, and in which on real water she would undoubtedly have tipped over. This large bronze for many years obscured the view of the street, as it was placed in our front window as was the style then in order that it might be seen by all passers by.

When I was a little girl Lake Michigan's waves lapped Michigan Avenue and there was a small breakwater just outside. We children used to walk on this breakwater; and one day I fell into the lake and was fished out by a by-stander, a very cold and frightened little girl. But the worst fright of my life occurred one day when I was looking underneath the sidewalk in front of my house. Chicago at that time had its sidewalks built, every one on a level of its own. When you walked up and down the street you went up and down innumerable steps and swept up the steps neatly with the long trains which were then the fashion in street clothes. I often made journeys of exploration underneath these sidewalks and one day I stumbled over something in the darkness. To my horror I found it was the body of a man. It later turned out that he had been murdered. After that day I kept to the open and left the intricate mazes of the streets under the sidewalks unexplored.

The horse and buggy was at this time the usual vehicle which Chicago people used for business, pleasure or shopping purposes. I remember one Sunday my father's telling me that a new park had just been opened on the North Side, and he took my mother and me in the buggy to see it. It was called Lincoln Park. It had been a grave yard, and as we drove through it we saw countless open graves with a piece here and there of a decayed coffin, and every now and then on a pile of dirt a bone, evidently dropped by those removing the bodies. The whole place looked exactly as if the Judgment Day had come, the trumpets had sounded and everyone had arisen from their graves, dropping now and then a little piece of their anatomy as they fled to Graceland or Rose Hill where they again deposited themselves underground. There was one tomb erected by the Couch family which had apparently refused to be removed and which still stands in Lincoln Park, hemmed in by bushes so that it is not perceptible to the passer by. I remember coming away from the park thinking that never would I be tempted to seek it for pleasure purposes, and in later years when I pleaded with Park trustees and officials to see that the Park was better lighted and more adequately policed because of the young people who frequented it, I often thought of my first glimpse of the place and the anything but pleasurable effect it produced upon my childish mind. Years later, when the house in which I now live was built, I can remember bones cropping up from the ground when the foundation was being dug. It had been used as a burial ground, and the first maids who came to me in that house said they were very doubtful about coming lest the people who had been buried in the basement would rise and haunt them.

As we stand now on Astor Street with its great shade trees on either side and its beautiful houses, and look north toward Lincoln Park, we find it difficult to realize that this street was once only a sandy beach which had been used as a cemetery.

I have lived for thirty-two years in my house on this street, it has been used at various times for all kinds of meetings, from Suffrage gatherings, where we were urging women to join the Suffrage ranks, to neighborhood meetings where we made appeals for the betterment of conditions in the ward.

We have had many dinners where some scheme of benefit to the City or County has been hatched out behind closed doors. The meetings have been held here in order not to have anyone know about them. I remember when my friend, Mr. Alexander A. McCormick, was made President of the County Board, he told me that he was most anxious to appoint good people as heads of the various County Departments, such as the Warden of the Hospital, the Head of the Social Service Department, etc., and that if we could suggest good people he would appoint them. I immediately called together about twenty-five people, heads of settlements, men interested in civic affairs, social workers, etc., and we sat all one evening trying to think of good men and women for the various county positions. One interesting thing was that in spite of all our efforts we were unable to select people for many of the County Institutions as the County did not pay a big enough salary to secure first class men. I remember what difficulty we had trying to think of a man who would head the County Hospital, as such a position required some one with experience and a genius for organization, and we were obliged to confess that we had utterly failed in thinking of anyone who could fill this position for the salary paid.

There were other dinners on the question of education where matters were coming up on the School Board which demanded immediate action by citizens.

Some of these plans which we formed at these dinners or meetings were sprung at large meetings held later and I have heard people say that they wondered where the plan originated but no one ever gave it away.

When a group of representative citizens come together and use their influence for the making of public opinion, it is not so difficult to swing a new project or a reform after a certain number of people have been secured as its backers. Unfortunately, one only has a limited number of interested citizens on whom to call in matters of this kind, too many people are indifferent to civic affairs, yet if every citizen could realize that the safety of his family, the honor of his wife and children, even his own happiness may be involved, we might be able to get more people who would be interested in gatherings of this kind.

CHAPTER II

A FASHIONABLE CAREER AND A FIRE

When I was about twelve years old I had a cousin visiting me from New York. She apparently lived in a round of fashion there and she was quite scornful of the fact that, in Chicago, the coachmen wore no livery and all the vehicles and horses were lacking in style. She told me of Fifth Avenue, with its rows of beautiful houses, its streets full of prancing horses and fine vehicles, with a footman and a coachman on every box, and of the pleasure of living amid such grandeur. I rose to the occasion and felt that I too must put on some style, but how to do it was the question.

We owned, as a family, at that time an old, rather battered-looking vehicle which was called a barouche; we had two horses, one rather larger than the other, and both looking somewhat down in the mouth. Their tails, their one glory, swept the ground, and their manes had not known a comb since they were colts. I particularly remember the barouche because, when I was five years old, I was taken for a drive in it, the horses became frightened and ran away and my grandmother, with great presence of mind, determined to drop me out of the little window in the back. This did not particularly appeal to me and I struggled so violently at being pushed through the small opening that the horses were finally brought to a standstill before the plan was consummated; therefore the barouche always gave me a most uncomfortable feeling.

The most prominent object about our turn-out was the coachman; he was a little Irishman named Barney, not over five feet tall, as ugly a man in appearance as I have ever seen, although kindly in disposition. He wore, as a general rule, a suit of light brown tweed with a dash of red in it. His necktie was almost always red, although I am sure he had never heard of an anarchist. He wore a soft felt hat, and as a crowning touch he almost always was smoking a short pipe which he deftly held on one side of his mouth, looking as if it were going to fall out. Added to this, being of a curious and literary turn of mind, he always read the newspaper when the trap was not moving.

On the whole, our equipage was as good as any in town. I would have been satisfied with it for many years had it not been for the ideas of style put into my mind by the New York cousin. Spurred on by her recriminations, I decided to be stylish and obtained permission from my father to spend my own money for a livery, if I cared to do so. I first interviewed Barney and told him that the cornerstone of such stylishness would have to be laid by a change of name for him; Barney sounded so very plebeian that in the future I would call him "Bernard." I also told him that thereafter he must call me Miss Louise. He objected only slightly to his own change of name but decidedly and positively refused to call me anything but "Lulu"—he said that was my name and he was not going to call me anything else. So "Lulu" it had to be, but I piously hoped that the New York cousin would never hear him.

I told Bernard that it was our duty to raise the standards for vehicles in Chicago and we must show that we had fine horses and equipages and coachmen who knew just as well as in New York what a correct turn-out was like. I finally enthused Bernard and he departed to look for a livery, although he hated the word; it "reminded him of slavery."

At that time a clothing firm in Chicago named Harvey had recently advertised liveries for sale. I told Bernard to get the nicest thing and not to spare expense—that we were going to dazzle the people of Chicago with our turn-out. I could hardly wait until he returned with his purchases. He came into the barn where I awaited him, a curious, comical little figure of an Irishman, simply snowed under with bundles, and said: "Lulu, when I seen them liveries with all the colors of the rainbow, I couldn't make up my mind which one you would like the best, and so I got two, one red and one blue." He then displayed the fruits of his labor and the liveries were lovely. One was bright blue with silver buttons and the other a dark red with gold buttons. We decided to keep both liveries, using the blue one on week days and the red one on Sundays and holidays. Then came the hat! It was a regulation stovepipe, but crowned with the largest cockade I have ever seen. We did not know at the time that cockades were used only by officials who were in the Navy. We were also undecided what collar and necktie were appropriate for this raiment but decided that the red necktie should be kept for the red livery and a blue one should be worn with the blue.

It was almost a weeping matter to cut the horses' tails. Bernard said they would die of the flies in the summertime and he said, "I don't know how I can look them horses in the face again if I cut off their fly-swatters," but he did it, keeping the hair from one flowing tail to be used as a switch in case of an emergency. Months later, when we were driving, on seeing one horse apparently shedding his tail I said: "Why, Bernard, that horse is losing his tail!" Bernard replied, "Don't fret, Lulu, it's only an extra switch I put on him to make his tail look bushier." Whereupon he calmly removed the tail and put it in his pocket.

Next, we plaited the horses' manes and tied them with red ribbon. There was no way of finding out (because my cousin had gone back to New York) whether this was stylish or not, but it seemed gay and appropriate, and I was so excited the first day the horses and carriage were ordered around to the front door that I could hardly wait to see them. Bernard was a magnificent figure. As soon as he arrived at the front of the house, attired in his blue livery and his cockade, he arose slowly from his seat and extracted from underneath it his pipe, and after he had lighted it produced a newspaper with which he proceeded to amuse himself. When I told him about making what I considered a smart appearance in front of the shops, I said that the pipe and newspaper would have to be relegated to the past, and he was then quite cross and whipped his horses so unmercifully that I was compelled to remonstrate.

I felt that on my first drive down Michigan Avenue in such splendor I wanted to try and not look above any acquaintance I might meet, and I was reminded of a story that my grandmother had told me about a friend of hers who, in the early days, owned a victoria and a pair of horses, and who at the same time had a new green silk dress. On the first day she went out attired in the dress and sitting in the victoria, in order not to have her townsfolk feel that she was proud and stuck-up, she purchased a bag of peanuts and ate them as she passed through the streets, carelessly throwing the shells right and left, to show that she could still enjoy common things.

About this time came the great Chicago fire. I was spending the winter in New York, and our first knowledge of it was a telegram from my father saying, "Chicago a mass of ruins; everything gone; I am safe." I walked out on Fifth Avenue that day and saw large wagons driving up and down the street with signs saying, "Give us clothes for the fire-sufferers." I can remember how doors opened and people ran out, throwing clothing of all kinds into the wagons. Later, when I returned to Chicago, my father met me at the station. I did not know him, for he was unshaven and had a fairly long beard. He wore no overcoat but had an old shawl over his shoulders. As we neared Chicago we passed large coal yards where great piles of coal were still burning. When we entered the city what struck me particularly was that we could see all over it—there was nothing to obstruct the view except an occasional chimney rising amid the ruins.

There was not a house standing on the South Side north of Harrison Street and not one on the North Side from the River to the Lake, until Lincoln Park was reached, with the exception of Mahlon Ogden's house, where the Newberry Library now stands.

Our own house on Michigan Avenue was not burned but it was full of people who had come to us for shelter. They were sleeping forty or fifty on the floor. The city was under martial law, General Sheridan in command. Most of the people in the city had not had their clothes off for a long time; some of them were patrolling the streets and alleys

CHICAGO IN FLAMES.

Published by Currier & Ives.

looking for incendiaries, of whom there were many about. The people at my house were eating up my pet bantams and cheerfully saying they did not mind their toughness. Our horses and my pony were doing good service in taking the people out to the country. My father told us his story of the fire; how he was asleep in the house of a friend on the North Side; hearing the fire bells he got up and saw that there was a great conflagration on the Southwest Side. The wind was blowing a gale and even then the sparks were falling all about the house. He dressed, woke some of the neighbors, and told them to watch out for their roofs, then went over town with his host, the president of the bank of which he was cashier. They reached Washington Street and started on a run for the bank, which was at the corner of Washington and LaSalle Streets. Flakes of fire were falling on the street, the court house opposite was in flames, the building in the rear of the bank was a burning mass. My father rushed into the building, found the two bank watchmen at their posts; with revolvers in their hands they rushed to the vaults and tried to open them. The combination was set on the word "Oats" and the president of the bank said in a grim way, "If my horse were here he could find this combination quicker than I." It seemed to them an age before the lock was set and the vault door opened. My father stepped inside, threw open the door of the safe, took from it all the currency, which was in packages, and removed several boxes of valuable securities; they then locked the vault and rushed for the street, where there had been a tremendous change in the few moments they had been in the bank. The fire was all over their heads, the air was full of burning brands, the heat was intense. With their hats crushed down over their faces, their coat collars turned up and boxes containing hundreds of thousands of dollars worth of securities in each hand, they rushed up the street, a watchman with a revolver keeping close to each one. A hackman stood on the corner of Dearborn Street. He was told his hack was wanted. He refused; a hundred dollars and then two hundred was offered, and the man could not resist the bribe. The men jumped in and were soon at the house of a friend on Michigan Avenue near Twenty-second Street, where they deposited their valuables. Then it dawned upon them that they must at once get to the North Side if they would save the women and children in the house where my father was visiting. The hackman had gone; they ran down Michigan Avenue from Twenty-second Street to Sixteenth Street, woke up a livery stable man, secured another hack and started down Michigan Avenue. It was an exciting ride. The driver was told to run his horses, that life and death were struggling together and that everything the president of the bank held most dear was at stake. My father said that, with his head out the window, he cried, swore and entreated in the same breath. It looked impossible when the hack reached Van Buren Street to go down Michigan Avenue, but it proved to be more smoke than flame. The horses did not want to go on but they were whipped through and finally came in sight of Rush Street's wooden bridge which was still standing but which was just beginning to burn. The other bridges had already gone, the great elevators on the North Side were in flames, and, from the time my father had been to the bank and down to Twenty-second Street, the fire had burned from the South Side far over to the North Side. They finally reached the house of the bank president, hurried to the stable, got out the horses, which they turned loose; then went into the house and got the women and children. The fire then was almost upon them; the wind was blowing a tremendous gale; great brands of fire were falling everywhere, even on the horses and carriage. Into the one hack in front of the door were put children and grown people, eleven in all; the driver, the bank president and my father on the box. After going a short distance they stopped to pick up an old woman who had rheumatism and was unable to walk. They finally went west on North Avenue to the West Side, then to the extreme South Side. It was a frightful night and my father was black as a chimney-sweep, his eyes scorched by the heat and his clothing burned in many places.

A little later General Sheridan caused some buildings on Michigan Avenue to be blown up and the flames were stopped. The timely aid sent by the surrounding cities prevented any suffering for food. St. Louis had seven carloads of provisions in Chicago before the fire ceased burning. The depression which existed a day or two following the fire was intense. No one knew whether bank vaults were burned or not; everyone felt that he was ruined but after a day or two people began to feel better, confidence gradually increased and by the time I returned to Chicago people were hopeful and cheerful, looking forward to the time when the city would arise from its ashes and be greater than ever before.

Everything was very simple after the fire. I was quite satisfied with the stylish appearance of our turn-out during the next five or six years, until my New York cousin visited me again. She had now become a very elegant young lady and said she never went out in New York without a footman on the box to open the door and to take her card in when she called. I felt that I must get a footman. My father told me to go ahead and get one if I wanted him, so I advertised. Unfortunately I did not call him a "footman" but a "groom." The first gentleman who appeared was a long, lanky youth from southern Illinois, who said he had long wanted to be a groom and have a wife, and he offered his services. I was much embarrassed and tried to explain that the groom I wanted was not a husband, and the would-be-groom departed much disappointed. I had no more applications for the same position, so I again advertised, this time for a "footman." The first to present himself in answer to this advertisement was a man so large that I did not feel there would be room on the box for him with Bernard, who was no sylph himself. I had great difficulty in getting rid of him as he assured me he was most agile in jumping up and down. However, I turned him away and hired a pale and anaemic youth, with a long golden mustache, whose name was Cornelius. This name sounded to me rather stylish and elegant. I did not want to go to the expense of a new livery, so I had him wear the red one (bought for Bernard before the fire, but still preserving its pristine freshness) as I thought the two men would present a variegated appearance on the box, one in red and one in blue. I couldn't find a cockade for Cornelius's hat as large as the one Bernard had, but thought this was of no importance.

The first day they drove around together on the box, I invited my mother to go for a drive and make some calls. It was a hot day in summer and I said to her, "It will be nice to have Cornelius ring the bell and take in our cards, and when we come out he can find our carriage for us." When our carriage left the front door it was a marvelous sight. The horses, with their manes tied up in red ribbons, seemed to have taken on an added splendor. Cornelius and Bernard in red and blue were quite startling and my mother and I, attired in our best clothes, felt that we looked very smart.

The first place at which we stopped to call, Cornelius got down rather heavily, and I entrusted him with our cards carefully turned down at the corner, as was the custom in those days to show you had called in person. I told him to ask for the friend on whom I was calling. Imagine my horror to see him remove his hat when the door was opened, and, after asking a question, vanish into the house. For one wild moment I thought of driving away and leaving him to his fate, but concluded to sit it out. At the end of ten minutes Cornelius emerged. When I haughtily said to him, "Where have you been?" he said, "The lady who opened the door asked me in, and I went upstairs and got in a room where a lady was dressing. She was angry, and told me to 'get out' and I got out." Mother and I did not stay to make that call.

We then went to another house and found the lady at home. When we came out I looked for Cornelius; he was not to be found. I walked half a block in the hot sun one way—no Cornelius; half a block in the sun another way—no Cornelius. Finally, on my third trip, I espied the carriage a block away under a tree, both men on the box, Bernard smoking a pipe and reading a newspaper, Cornelius smoking a cigar and reading a novel. I had to poke him in the back with my parasol before

I could attract his attention. I felt then that I had a great work of reform to accomplish.

Later on, as I grew older and longed for more stylish fields to conquer, I bought myself a two-wheeled cart where the driver and groom sat dos-a-dos. By this time my groom was wearing top boots and I had great difficulty in getting men who were willing to wear what they called "only their underdrawers" with boots over them. On one occasion I was delighted to engage a little German. When I told him he would have to wear top boots, he told me he always wore them and had a pair of his own. I was much pleased, and the first time he brought the trap around to the door, I found to my horror that he had on a pair of Hessian boots which came up to his waist. Another time my groom told me he would have to have a pair of trees to put his breeches on to dry after they had been washed because they shrank so badly. I was quite indignant at this expenditure, and asked him why he could not let them dry on him. He was so provoked at my asking him to thus "catch his death of cold" that he gave notice at once. My dog cart attracted much attention, so much, indeed, that every little boy who saw it threw something at it to show his appreciation. Stones and rotten eggs were not at all uncommon, and at one time I was two days in bed from being struck in the ear with a stone. Naturally I found it rather difficult to get a man who was willing to risk his life as my footman. On one occasion my man was driving with me across the Rush Street Bridge. He said to me, "Are you going over town, Miss?" I haughtily replied, "I certainly am," whereupon he said, "I am not going with you; you may take my livery but you cannot take me." With that he got off the cart (on the bridge) pulled off his coat, flung it onto the back of the cart, took off his hat and pitched it after the coat, removed each glove, then collar and necktie, and left me driving away with the empty husk, the livery but not the man. It was an humiliating experience, and one that was greeted with jeers of derision for me by those who witnessed the incident, and with cheers for the groom "who would not be made a slave."

It seemed almost a necessity to have a second person on the box in these early days, because when you gave an entertainment it was not considered stylish, or even civil, to send an invitation through the mails. It had to be delivered in person, not merely sent by a messenger; moreover it was not considered the thing to have the invitations engraved, printed or typed—they had to be written by hand. Before giving a party whole days had to be spent in writing invitations, stacking them up in boxes by streets, then the hostess to be drove around with the invitations, and they were delivered by a footman or messenger who sat on the box with the coachman.

It was quite an undertaking to entertain when I

was young. The invitations having been sent out, the next thing to do was to clean the house very thoroughly. No matter how clean it *had* been, it must be cleaned because you were going to have company. First the large Nottingham lace curtains were taken down and carefully washed. As we did not have any curtain-stretchers, they were pinned down to the carpets in every hall and bedroom in the house. The curtains had points, and each point had three pins which were an endless chore to put in; my knees were sore and my hands ached from pressing them, and there was an odor of starch and general cleanliness throughout the house.

In every room where curtains were pinned to the floor it was only possible to walk by putting one foot in front of the other, down little aisles between the curtains. I used to pretend that the curtains were the water and the little aisles the land; occasionally I slipped and a dirty shoe went into the curtain when the spot had to be washed out and the curtain stretched down again.

Then the crystal chandeliers had to be washed. Mounted on a stepladder, I carefully took down every little dangler (amounting in my estimation to several million), handed them to my mother, and she washed them in hot suds, carefully breathed upon them and polished them with a chamois, then handed them back to me. I took them, breathed on them, polished them with a chamois and hung them on the chandelier. It was a great undertaking and took more patience than I possessed. When I was told I could have a party I sometimes wondered if the pleasure I got out of it was worth the washing of the crystal chandelier.

Finally came the day of the party. We arose at six o'clock because all the food had to be prepared at home, as caterers' food was not then considered either good or stylish. The oysters were carefully looked over to be sure there were no shells; the chicken and celery for the salad were cut in little squares, it being almost a heinous offense to have one piece larger than the other. A large perfectly new washtub was bought for the mixing of the salad. Bernard, grown quite fat and puffing from exertion, froze freezer after freezer of ice cream; we made rolls and sponge cake, and as we toiled in the kitchen Cornelius struggled with heavy canvas which he tacked down over the carpets, afterwards donning his livery, and with white gloves on his hands opening the door for the expected guests.

During the afternoon there were many inquiries, such as, "Is this a large enough party to wear a dress suit?" or "Shall girls wear party dresses?" or "Shall we arrive at prompt eight o'clock?" Finally, when eight o'clock came and the guests began to arrive, those of us who had worried to get the house clean and the supper ready, were so tired we could hardly stand up.

Chicago was a delightful summer watering place. When hot weather came the drawing room was moved to the front steps. It was a poverty-stricken family that did not have its stoop rug put out every evening at dark, on which the younger members of the family sat and talked while the elders occupied rocking chairs in the vestibule.

About this time there was a craze for archery. It was said to be a noble sport which came down to us from Merrie England, and I was enraptured with it. I bought myself a very large bow, so large I could hardly manage it; a quiver full of dangerous looking arrows, an arm guard, to prevent my skinning my arm, a finger and a thumb guard; a rakish little cap which made me think I looked like Robin Hood, and a tarlatan plaid skirt, which I thought the proper costume. I decided to give an archery party. There was a place at the north of the house suitable for a target and space enough to shoot a long distance. One sultry afternoon guests began to arrive; I led them forth to the side yard where the target was set up. They tried to pull my bow, but their aim went very wild, and finally, as I had had a good deal of practice, I modestly took the bow to show what I could do. I had three arrows, two of which missed the target, and one managed to hit the end of it. A little girl who was acting as my factotum, kindly ran toward the target to bring back the arrows, but one was not to be found. The target was just in front of a small yard where the family cow was taking her siesta. Imagine my dismay when the factotum, after looking over the fence, came back screaming, "The other arrow is in the cow!" True enough, it had missed the target, gone over the fence and landed in the poor cow. After that I did not take so much interest in archery, which seemed to me a very old-fashioned sport.

One of the great social events of the year was the celebration of New Year's Day. Every man, young or old, from the callow youth to the aged beau, made calls on that day. Hacks were pressed into service, and these rickety vehicles would disgorge often as many as eight callers. It was the custom for four or five girls to receive together, but the day began early. There was only one hairdresser on the North Side at that time, so it was difficult to secure her, and I remember rising at 5 a. m. to have my hair dressed with a mass of puffs, feeling very sleepy as I tried to take another nap before breakfast. Then there was the making of chicken salad, the roasting of turkeys, the mixing of egg-nog, the setting of the table, and the getting of everything ready for the visitors. They began to arrive at 10 a. m., and continued until 10 p. m., a steady stream ascending the steps of almost every house in town. Each girl kept a list of her visitors, and brought it forth in triumph the following day, to show how many calls she had received. If there was a death in the family a small basket tied with white ribbon hung on the bell-knob, and into this basket cards were dropped by the callers.

Sleigh rides were very popular at this time, not the "twosing" cutter, but long, low, racy-looking sleighs filled with hay and a mass of buffalo robes. They were packed with people to an almost unbelievable extent. We sat on the seats, on the sides, on the hay, on each other's laps, and we usually drove north to the house of a friend for a supper and a dance. The following invitation lingers in my memory:

"If on Friday the Third there is snow on the ground,
And no meteorological obstacles found,
Miss de Koven requests you will give her the pleasure—
A pleasure, believe her, words cannot measure,
Of your company then at a small sleighing party,
Where friends you will meet and a welcome quite hearty.
She asks you to come at half after eight,
When a sleigh with four horses will wait at her gate.
The party goes northward, to sup and to dance,
With sleigh bells that ring and horses that prance,
To be fed from the cupboard of kind Mrs. Hubbard.
Please send a reply and be sure to appear
With frolic and sleigh bells to greet the New Year."

The Mrs. Hubbard referred to in the above invitation was Mrs. Elijah K. Hubbard, who lived just northwest of the Park on Diversey Avenue. This was considered quite a long sleigh ride; so long, in fact, that it was necessary to stop for a time in order to rest the horses.

In spite of all the fatigue in getting up entertainments of this kind, I am sure that everyone had a better time than at modern entertainments where the only trouble involved is interviewing musicians and caterers, and I am convinced that the most fashionable parties given in Chicago now do not compare for pure enjoyment with the parties given after the fire by the most fashionable club of Chicago called "The Cinders." This club met in Martine's Hall on Chicago Avenue, and everyone who was fortunate enough to secure an invitation to it had a most delightful time. We were, perhaps, rather countrified in those days, but we prided ourselves on knowing how to do the correct thing, and we were all a bit shocked at one big private supper party to have quill toothpicks passed with the coffee, each quill bearing the inscription "Presented by Kingsley," the caterer who had furnished the entertainment.

After all, if we *were* countrified, we had certain standards and ideals which we all tried to live up to and which certainly made for sterling character and sound citizenship. There was no liquor served at any of the parties given in Chicago in these early days, and a young man ever seen under the influence of it was never invited anywhere again.

Perhaps, if in the midst of our present wild rush after pleasure, we gave a thought to those early days and adopted some of the standards then in vogue, we might have just as good a time and some of the tragedies in our social life might be averted.

CHAPTER III

CHURCH, HOSPITALS AND NURSES

I always went to church every Sunday with my parents. We lived on the South Side, and we drove north in a buggy, the horse being hitched while we were at church. After church I always lunched at the house of my Sunday School teacher to whom I was passionately devoted.

I was also allowed to help my mother, who was chairman of the Chancel Committee, and every Sunday I assisted her in arranging two vases of flowers for the altar, finding the Lessons for the day and, during the week, mending the cassocks worn by the boy choir. Later I was made chairman of this Committee, and every Easter, Christmas and Holy Day I was at church at five or six o'clock in the morning to get my work done and floral decorations in place before the early service at eight o'clock. It was perhaps good discipline for a young girl thus to get up early and to have responsibility, but I was always very sleepy and tired before night.

The church at that time was the only outlet for social work. The girls taught in sewing and Sunday schools, they visited the poor, they trimmed the church at Christmas and Easter. This church trimming was a matter of great importance, and work began two or three weeks before Christmas, as the greens had to be made into wreaths. The work was done in the basement of the church, and so absorbed the attention of all the young people in the parish that no social entertainment was given during the two weeks preceding Christmas. The young men were always on hand in the evenings to help with the heavy work. It was, altogether, a joyful time. Later in life, when I had had a good deal of experience in social work, I had a pang of conscience that I was doing no church work. I went to my rector and asked for something to do. After thinking the matter over he offered me the chairmanship of the Chancel Committee, the same work I had done when I was an inexperienced girl. This work I declined on the ground that my experience should have fitted me for something more responsible.

When I was sixteen years old I felt I ought to take a Sunday School class, and one Sunday afternoon, with much sinking of the heart, I presented myself to the superintendent of the Sunday School and asked for a class. He told me that there was none without a teacher that day except a class of big boys which had been given up the former week, because their teacher felt she could not manage them. Disappointed that I was not to teach, I asked if I could not try this class of bad boys. I was told that I could, but that they were quite unmanageable. When I was escorted to the class the boys sat in a semi-circle around me; my heart failed me as they were boys of fourteen and sixteen years of age, very rough looking, and certainly very rough acting. I was consoled, however, by the fact that the sons of the sexton, the rector of the parish, and the bishop of the diocese were in the class. To my disappointment, however, they did not prove to be a soothing factor. When I sat down I said I had never had a class before and knew nothing of the rules of the school, but that I intended to be obeyed and that I would not tolerate any rough-housing—that any boy who was not quiet I would put out of the room. One big boy immediately kicked the boy next to him. I told him to be quiet, but as he kicked again I thought it was time for action, and seizing the big boy by the collar I pulled him off the bench and out into the aisle down toward the door, which, when I reached, I opened and cast him out. The whole affair was so unexpected—that is, being seized by a girl and dragged down the aisle before the whole school—that the boy did nothing but kick, but as I was a strong young person I had no difficulty in putting him out. When I returned to the class everyone was as quiet as a mouse. I began the lesson, and from that time on I never had one bit of trouble with the boys. I held this Sunday School class for eleven years. The boys grew into young men, but stayed with me, and brought in others until I had a class of one hundred. The Sunday School room was too small for them, and I had them in the transept of the church itself. I always had the lesson and then told a story which illustrated somewhat, or was intended to illustrate, the subject on which I had been talking. I called the class "The Soldiers of Christ," and if a boy was perfect in attendance and deportment for three months he had a yellow card given him, stating that he had been made a Corporal in the "Soldiers of Christ"; six months made him a Sergeant, nine months a third Lieutenant, etc., and when he became a General he received a gold watch.

When I was holding the class in the transept of the church, the body of the church was occupied by deaf mutes who were holding their regular service there. It was very upsetting to see them rise, kneel and pray, and go through the ritual of the Episcopal Church, and I was always glad to see the clergyman begin his sermon, because then it was less confusing and I did not feel we were interrupting. One day these deaf mutes were, by mistake, locked in the chapel; being unable to make any sound, they spent the night there before they were discovered.

I found that the young men in my class had very little opportunity for recreation, and I had them at my house three times a week to play billiards with me in the billiard room which was in the basement of the house. I also tried to keep in close touch with the boys, so visited their families frequently, heard their troubles and learned to know something about them from their parents. As the boys grew older I found places for them when they went to work. I almost ran an employment agency, for any young man that I knew who did not send to me the information that the store or firm in which he worked wanted a boy never heard the last of it, and I made myself a great nuisance to my friends. I have never experienced in any other way the satisfaction I felt when I was told that some boy I had placed had made good and was promoted. When one boy who had promised well stole something and would have been sent to the penitentiary had it not been for my interference, I was quite broken-hearted. On the whole, the boys did very well, and not long ago I had a letter from one of them telling me that he wanted an appointment as Federal Judge, and hoped to get it.

My billiard room was so unequal to accommodating the young men who came to my house that I determined to find a club house for them. I accordingly secured an old studio on Huron Street which had two large rooms downstairs that were used for lounge and card rooms, and two rooms upstairs for billiard and pool rooms. I put the place in good order, furnished it and found a man who said he would take care of it and be there every night; and this was the first boys' club, to my knowledge, in Chicago. Later I built a large club for boys at Hull-House, fitted up with shops, games and pool rooms, and every convenience, but this club never gave me the real pleasure I got out of the Huron Street Club, which seemed to be all my own. This club was kept up until after I was married and my children were born. During this period I had not been able to devote much time to it, and it seemed best to abandon it as there was no one to take charge of it.

While I was a Sunday School teacher I was also a teacher in the sewing school. I knew very little about sewing and when I was given my first class I found that they were making flannel petticoats, and in my ignorance I had them sew up each side of the petticoat, so that there was no way of getting into it.

One day some money had been missed from the collection plate at sewing school, and I was told by the superintendent that I must search each child to see if it could be found. This was such a disagreeable undertaking that I gave up the sewing school and never returned to it.

Later on, with Eleanor Ryerson, I heard of the Kitchen Garden Association—of its great usefulness—and we determined to start one in Chicago in connection with the church. We were given the chapel for our labors, and every Saturday we had about one hundred little girls to whom we taught domestic work. The Kitchen Garden consisted of an equipment of little beds about large enough for a big doll. These were fitted up with sheets, pillows, blankets, etc. Then there were brooms and dusters, little tables and chairs, all kinds of dishes for the table, with forks, spoons and knives and all sorts of kitchen utensils. The idea of the Kitchen Garden was to teach children how to do housework and to do it so pleasantly and correctly that the knowledge thus acquired would stay by them all their lives. Each occupation, whether it was bed-making, dusting, cooking or table-setting and waiting, was accompanied by songs, and the children went through their little drills with great exactness.

The real trouble with the system was that the homes of the children did not have the perfect beds nor the complete equipment which was furnished them in miniature so the system sometimes failed to work. We kept up this Kitchen Garden Association, raising money for it and doing it on a large scale, until it was finally taken over by the public schools, after we had given frequent demonstrations of it and brought much influence to bear to have it adopted.

This Kitchen Garden Association was only one of the many experiments made by a private organization which, having proved their worth, have been taken over and made a part of city or county activities.

During this time there was very little outlet for anyone who was interested in social work. I had been brought up with the idea that some day I would inherit a fortune, and I was always taught that the responsibility of money was great, and that God would hold me accountable for the manner in which I used my talents. I was, therefore, most eager to learn how to spend what I had in a proper way. My visiting among the hundred families of my Sunday School boys had become so extensive and so many demands for help came to me that I felt I must have some assistance. The old Relief and Aid Society was functioning and it gave aid to worthy people, but did not follow up nor attempt any rehabilitation of the family, and I always had a very strong feeling that something must be done to put a family upon its feet and not just to give temporary aid. I, therefore, employed a Swedish widow whom I knew, and when I had a call for help she would visit the family and try to do very much as the modern investigators for the United Charities do today. She found where the man of the family worked, what he was earning, looked after the health of the children, showed the mother how to purchase, and how to spend her money economically, gave advice on home keeping matters, and then reported to me the sum she thought the family needed, either temporarily or as a permanent stipend. She worked for me in this way for several years, and although she never had any instructions in modern methods of administering relief, yet she had rare common sense, was a good housekeeper, and had the practical experience which enabled her to judge wisely in giving assistance.

I was twenty-seven years old when I was married, and my four children were born during the next six years. I missed the visits I had formerly made among the families of my Sunday School class. When I was making these visits, up and down the most disreputable streets of the North Side, climbing over ash heaps and piles of garbage into old buildings in back yards, I often felt that when I had more money of my own, some of it would be spent in erecting homes for the poor.

After the fire, Chicago was almost immediately rebuilt with little wooden shanties about as close together as it was possible to put them, with no plumbing and no conveniences; only outhouses under the high sidewalks—not only most inconvenient, but in every way most unsanitary. Not many years later I wanted to build a model tenement in which people, for a moderate rent, could have some degree of comfort. I took an option on a square block of land and my architect prepared some plans; however, when they were finished and the estimates for the building began to come in, I found I could only secure about a 2½% return on my investment, and as what I had in mind was to demonstrate that model tenements could be erected and make a return to the owner of at least 4%, it hardly seemed worth while to continue, and I most reluctantly gave up the plan and joined with some other people in building a small model tenement for Hull-House Association.

During this time I had visited all the model tenements in New York City; talked with housing experts generally, and had tried to inform myself concerning the best kind of building to be erected. My attention had been particularly turned toward the beautiful tenements then recently erected in Germany, where the building itself was a pleasure to the eye, where broad hallways, large windows, fine balconies and spacious grounds made the buildings most habitable, and where the working man could obtain for his children the light, the air and the sunshine which is theirs by right.

It was a great disappointment to me to give up the building of a model tenement, and I began to look about me for something else with which to occupy my time. With my children so young, I could not be away from home very much, so I became a member of the Board of Managers of the Maurice Porter Memorial Hospital, an institution for sick children founded and supported by Mrs. Julia Porter, and erected by her in memory of a child she had lost. I was shortly after made president of the board of this hospital, and found the work very engrossing and most distressing. To see little children suffer, to see them put into casts, so often necessary, to hear them wailing for their mothers, was something I could hardly bear. After being connected with the hospital three or four years I built a wing to it, housing about twenty-five more children. I remember one day before

Christmas taking my children to the hospital and my eldest boy, then about ten years old, gave an exhibition of legerdemain, in one of the wards. The children were so interested and so pathetic in their eagerness to try the tricks he showed them.

On another occasion I took my four children to the hospital and, as usual, I entered the front door without ringing. As we were going up the stairs we met a sad little procession coming down, two men carrying the coffin of a child. A frantic nurse from the upper hall was waving her arms and calling to us "Go away: That child has just died of malignant diphtheria!" We had rather an anxious Christmas, but fortunately no one developed any illness.

Later on, the hospital did not go very well. We had a great many empty beds; parents complained that members of the medical board were not giving their children sufficient attention. The physicians on the board replied there were so few children at the hospital that it was not worth while to go there. After many conferences between the medical board and the directors of the hospital, I summoned my directors and told them I thought the only thing to do was to dismiss the medical board and get a new one. They agreed, and Dr. Albert J. Ochsner was asked if he would head the new board. He said he would, and he would guarantee the hospital would be filled. A polite letter was written by the board of directors dismissing the medical board, and Dr. Ochsner was to take charge the following week. Just at this time I was called East on business, and while I was gone my directors became exceedingly uneasy over the fact that they were only going to "nurse Swedish children" in the hospital. They arrived at this conclusion because Dr. Ochsner was head of the Augustana Hospital which had a large clientele of Swedish people. The board did not trouble to communicate with me, but advised Dr. Ochsner that there would be no change in the medical board; they apologized to their own medical board and asked them to resume their duties. A few weeks later I resigned, feeling it was the wisest course under the circumstances. Later the hospital came under the charge of Mrs. Russell Tyson, who was made president of it. She did most marvelous work with it, and built it up in a remarkable manner, raising money for it and securing a large endowment, so now, housed in its new building, under the name of the Children's Memorial Hospital, it plays a most important part in the hospital life of the city.

Having had a taste of hospital management and not being at all discouraged by my downfall at the Porter Hospital, I became a member and vice president of the Woman's Board of St. Luke's Hospital. Mrs. E. S. Stickney was president at that time, and as she was not well, I was the acting head. I was, however, disturbed by the fact that my meetings had to be opened with prayer, and I never felt quite at home in my capacity as a leader.

Later I became president of the Woman's Board of the Passavant Hospital, a most homelike little place on Superior Street. This hospital did a great deal of charity work among the poor. A spirit of kindness and cheer just radiated throughout the building; the nurses were always most kind and sympathetic, and I have never seen anyone who received attention there who did not speak of it with tears of thankfulness. I went to this hospital almost every day; visited the wards, looked into private rooms, inspected the trays, tasted the food, talked with the nurses and superintendent, and did what I could to contribute to its moral and physical welfare.

My experience in visiting the poor had shown me how much they needed the ministrations of a trained person when they were ill. I had visited many children who were not well cared for by their parents, and who so much needed nursing and scientific care. I remember one day being very much distressed by going into a house built in the rear of a yard; I climbed up a long flight of wooden stairs on the outside of the house, and was then taken through a kitchen where at least twenty women sat making buttonholes and sewing on buttons on countless pairs of trousers which were piled in heaps on table and chairs. For this work these women received a beggarly pittance.

The mother whom I had gone to see, took me into a bedroom which was perfectly dark, and on the bed, covered with newspapers, lay a little child so emaciated that it seemed as though her bones were sticking through her skin. On a chair by the bed was a lighted candle, the only light in the room, and beside it lay a hunk of bread, the child's food for the day. The little girl, with dirty face, matted and unkempt hair, was holding in her clawlike fingers a long iron spike which she was dressing in a soiled piece of tissue paper and which she told me was her doll. If that child could only have had a visiting nurse she would have been much more comfortable, and with this incident in mind I was very glad to go to a meeting a little later, held at the house of Mrs. John R. Lyon on Michigan Avenue, where a number of us formed the Visiting Nurse Association of Chicago, that fine charity, whose ministering fingers have been laid in sympathy and healing on thousands of our sick poor.

I was a member of this association for many years, at first on the nurses committee, interviewing and engaging nurses, talking to them of their duties, and trying to put a standard before them of what their work ought to be, urging upon them the patience, the sympathy, the kindness, and above all the tact, which they must use in every household which they visited.

Later we began to hear about the school nurses in the East and we found that the first school nurses in the country, in connection with medical inspection, had been put on by the Henry Street Settlement in New York. Before the establishment of these nurses 24,538 children had been excluded from the public schools in a year. The nurses so demonstrated their usefulness (only 400 children being excluded the following year) that they were adopted by the New York Department of Health in 1902.

Early in the year 1906, Miss Jane Addams, who was then Chairman of the School Management Committee of the Chicago Board of Education, had that body confer with members of the Visiting Nurse Association for the purpose of securing the services of some visiting nurses in the schools in order that they might prevent the spread of contagious diseases, reduce truancy, and cure many of the little ills to which neglected children are so subject. Finally an appropriation was made from "The Paula Holmes Grey Memorial Fund." This provided for the support of two nurses, and I offered to furnish the third. These nurses worked for three months in the public schools and then were discontinued, but in 1907 they were put on again by the city under the supervision of the Visiting Nurse Association, and this time in larger numbers. The nurses were then able to detect physical defects in children so that their ailments did not become chronic, and when the medical inspectors sent children home from school suffering from minor troubles, the school nurse would immediately call, and take a hand in administering the remedy prescribed by the medical inspector. These nurses were paid only $600.00 a year and, among my old speeches, I find one given before the Finance Committee of the City Council, when I asked that their salaries be raised to $750.00 a year.

As a member of the Visiting Nurse Board I was put in charge of the school nurses, and continued this work for some time. I was always anxious to know exactly what the nurses were doing and, therefore, frequently accompanied them on their rounds. Some of the cases we visited were so awful and so startling that I sometimes wondered if the school nurse had not prepared a specially bad number of cases for me to see. I remember one kitchen in the cellar of a dirty tenement; when the nurse opened the door the stench was unbelievable. Five children, all naked except for little cotton undershirts, literally wallowed in three or four inches of filth; they were thin and scrawny and pot-bellied, and looked more like the pictures we have recently seen of the starving children of the Near East than the children of people living in a great and prosperous city.

Another case I visited just before Christmas, the mother said she was making soup for the children, and when I looked into the pot to see what was in it, I found it full of empty spools on which white thread had been wound. The mother was a seamstress, poorly paid; having no food for the children she was boiling some water and flavoring it with the wooden spools. When, in my ignorance, I sent them the next day a turkey, and then called to see how they had enjoyed it, I was horrified to see the bird dressed up in one of the children's dresses and put in the only bed in the place to keep it warm. Upon inquiry I found they did not have an oven in which to cook the turkey and, being foreigners, did not understand the eatableness of the bird, and, therefore, used it for a plaything. By the time I saw my gift, it was in a stage of decomposition and required to be promptly removed. I learned several lessons from this incident.

Another case which I remember with great vividness, was one where three children were ill with scarlet fever in a dingy dark room on the third story of a house, and I had visions, as I was taken into this room, of all my own children coming down with the same dreadful disease.

We found one boy of twelve years who was doing the housework for a family of eight. This boy was causing his teacher great anxiety as, at the afternoon session of school, he seemed to sink into a stupor and it was difficult to arouse him; even when this was accomplished he seemed vague for some time. The school nurse, after much questioning, secured the information that he did not go home at noon, but did errands for a saloon, receiving as pay a free luncheon consisting of beer and bread, the latter he soaked in whiskey and ate, a situation calculated to produce stupor, if nothing worse, in a child of his age.

The school nurses were often able to find the causes for mysterious ailments and sometimes the reason proved most ludicrous. I remember one boy who attended school regularly and although he appeared to be very clean, he had such an unpleasant odor about him that the children refused to sit near him. Questions asked the boy as to his personal habits, showed that he bathed frequently. Finally the school nurse was sent to investigate. She found that the family had recently moved into new quarters; they had kept a goat in the back yard of their old home, but not having a yard in the new one, they kept the goat in the same room with the boy, and this close proximity to the animal did not tend to make the boy resemble a violet. The family were told they must get along without the goat if the boy was to continue his education.

In another house all the children had pediculosis. The stepmother objected to the nurse's treatment, saying that nothing could be done for the children because they had inherited this trouble from their mother who had died nine years before.

Another instance showed that it is not always safe for physicians to use scientific names when talking to their patients. One woman whom I knew and who lived in a congested part of the city, telephoned me to say that she was in great trouble. Her daughter did not seem well and she had taken her to a physician who said she had tuberculosis and advised head treatment. The woman said she felt sure tuberculosis was not in her daughter's head as she had such splendid hair, and she wanted to know what to do. I immediately replied that I would send her to see the best tuberculosis specialist in Chicago, and I would anxiously await his report. The next day the specialist called me up. He was rather irate, saying the girl I had sent to him had been examined in his office and there was nothing the matter with her except pediculosis, but that she had a bad case, and that her head must be treated at once. I went to see the mother and carefully explained the situation, congratulating her that she had misunderstood the scientific term used for the disease, and that there was really nothing serious the matter with her daughter. Much to my surprise she was very much disappointed, feeling that at least tuberculosis was a high-toned trouble, while pediculosis was most vulgar and commonplace. I had some difficulty in persuading her to begin immediately the necessary treatment.

I am reminded of these incidents because at a meeting of the Visiting Nurse Association where I reported for the school nurses and told these stories, I was followed by Dr. George Vincent who, when he rose to speak, said he had listened with great pleasure to the zoological and entomological discourse of Mrs. Bowen. The audience laughed greatly at my expense, in which I heartily joined.

These school nurses were paid by the Visiting Nurse Association, but that association was constantly trying to prove to the municipality that the expense of them should be assumed by the Health Department. Statistics were gathered to the effect that the nurses in the last three months of 1908 had made 3,497 visits to the public schools, 17,039 visits to children in their homes, and there had been a noticeable decrease in truancy; contagious diseases were less, and communicable diseases much more controlled. The Board of Education was so impressed by these figures and these reports that they took over the entire staff of school nurses and have continued them in increasing numbers ever since. While the city's standard of efficiency was not so high as that set by the Visiting Nurse Association, nor the nurses so well supervised as when under the control of that body, still on the whole the work was fairly well done by the city. Since that time there have been frequent rumors and threats that the school nurses were to be given up; at one time thirty of them were discharged, and the remaining forty were given a month's notice. The women then, as now, rallied to the support of the cause to which they had devoted so much of their time, and the nurses were allowed to remain. They have gone through many vicissitudes, have had incompetent supervisors and incompetent heads of the Health Department, but on the whole it is a distinct gain and it was an achievement of the Visiting Nurse Association to convince the city, by practical illustration, that school nurses were necessary and to make the city assume the responsibility.

The Illinois Training School for Nurses was started about this time. Later on this school was directed by Mrs. Ira Couch Wood, to whom this book is dedicated, a brilliant young woman whose interest in civic affairs was most remarkable, and who as director of the Elizabeth McCormick Memorial Fund, devoted her life to the health and welfare of children.

Under the management of Mrs. Wood, the training school became so efficient that it furnished well-trained nurses in an ever-increasing number, for the expanding needs of the city.

No doubt the excellent reputation Chicago enjoys as one of the healthiest cities in the world is due to the fact that not only the early settlers, but those who succeeded them, realized the necessity of preventive measures, if they wished to retain the health of the vigorous people who started Chicago.

CHAPTER IV

THE UNITED CHARITIES

When I took a walk I liked to go into the poorer parts of the town and see what was going on, especially in my own ward. I used to walk often in the western part of what was then the 21st ward in a neighborhood known as "Little Hell" where the streets and sidewalks were so full of children that it was difficult to make your way among them. These were mostly the children of the Sicilians who had settled in this neighborhood. Because of economic pressure in Southern Italy and the fact that they had been ruthlessly exploited from the time that they landed at Ellis Island, they found themselves with very little money, and were obliged to guard their resources, and even to pool them with other families. They rented unsanitary tenements or old fashioned houses with damp cellars and rotten woodwork and defective plumbing, or they crowded together in a few rooms where it was impossible to observe even the common decencies of life. The men were unskilled laborers, taking what work they could get, and paying the larger part of their first month's salaries to the employment bureau which had secured them their position. They were mostly working digging on the streets or on the railroads, or making excavations for buildings. The women, who had never been accustomed to any modern appliances, did not know how to use our wash tubs or stoves, and most of them became garment finishers, for which they received the smallest kind of wage. I often met them staggering along the streets at dusk under the weight of dozens of pairs of men's trousers or coats which they were taking home to work upon, and which they were adding to the litter of the already overcrowded rooms.

This was before Illinois under the leadership of Mrs. Florence Kelly, was able to secure the Anti-Sweat Shop Law which provided that no work of this kind could be done in homes, a piece of legislation which has not only protected the wearers of cheap clothing, but which has been an inestimable boon to the workers themselves.

Sometimes I went further north to walk through a district known as Smoky Hollow, comprising something like 150,000 people made up of Italians and Irish, and another locality, then called "Goose Island," which was largely Polish. I was so much interested in these people and in what was being done for them that I became a member of the advisory committee of the Bureau of Charities which later became the United Charities. I was later made chairman of this committee, and for twelve years sat every Thursday morning at the office on North Wells Street, hearing the stories of the families who through the preceding week had applied for assistance, and deciding what was best to be done for them. These mornings were always most depressing, not only because of the abject tale of human misery which was poured into our ears, but because the resourcefulness and ingenuity and judgment and sympathy of the committee were taxed to the utmost. Financial assistance was often needed, and while the society could obtain the free services of doctors, nurses, dispensaries and hospitals, and while it had free access to almost all the institutions in the city and was able to purchase many things at wholesale rates, yet rent, fuel and food had to be paid for in cash. As chairman, I often had to make appeals to people in my district and while a few most generously responded, I was more often met with polite refusals. The United Charities now has ten such district offices, each one with its superintendent and assistants—each one an oasis of helpfulness in the midst of a desert of wretchedness. The procedure in all of the offices is the same. An applicant enters and asks for assistance. She is received by the superintendent, who listens to her story, sympathizes and promises to send a visitor. If it is an emergency case, and hunger and cold have already entered the home, an order for fuel and food is given at once. Then a trained worker is sent to the house whose experience enables her to judge what has led to the present difficulty, and perhaps to suggest plans for its abatement. Temporary aid is given and some time during the week the story comes before the advisory committee who look at the problem from all sides, try to get into communication with relatives and friends, find employment for members of the family, move them to more sanitary quarters, send the sick to hospitals or dispensaries, take the parents who are neglecting their children into court, remove those suffering from tuberculosis to places where they can have an opportunity to recover and not infect others, bring back deserting husbands to deserted wives, teach mothers the values of foods so that for less cost they may give their children a more nutritious diet, or, if there is no means of support, get the mother a pension from the Juvenile Court that will keep the family together until perhaps the children are old enough to work. There seems to be no limit to what a district office tries to do. It acts as trustee, guardian, advisor or friend. It will even, through the friendly visitors, do the housekeeping for families. All of these district offices have connected with them men and women, mostly women, in comfortable circumstances, who are willing to give up their time and their strength to visit the families of the poor, to advise, to sympathize and to cheer, for in many instances we find that in the families of foreign people unaccustomed to our methods of living and discouraged by their inability to make the adjustment and adapt themselves to the life here, they become discouraged and careless and sometimes even criminal. Often a friend who takes an interest in them and who shows her real desire to be of service, acts as a tonic, so that the family, in their desire to please and to show their gratitude, pull themselves together and rehabilitate themselves in a striking manner.

Sometimes fate seemed to be relentless almost to the point of absurdity, as in one case I remember of an Italian family who seemed to be happy and prosperous. The man was riding on a street car and was suddenly assaulted by an irate passenger, it being a case of mistaken identity. His nose was broken and he was badly disfigured. He sued for damages, but could not recover anything. A few days later, on his way from the dispensary where he had been to get his wound dressed, he fell off a sidewalk and broke his leg. The mother gave birth to a child the same day. Another child died the following day, and the eldest girl, only fourteen years old, who had been sent to look for work, was foully assaulted on the street. One could almost concur in the South Italian superstition that the evil eye had been cast upon this family.

Sometimes the demands for help upon our committee had a most gruesome as well as comical side. I remember one morning a small boy coming into the office, saying that his mother was dead, and that his uncle had pulled out his dead mother's tooth, and had gone away with it. On asking the boy why anyone had committed such a desecration of the dead, the reply was that "Mother has a diamond set in her front tooth and uncle wanted to sell it." Inquiry followed, which resulted in the information that in the mother's earlier days she had been an actress, and in order to make her smile more dazzling she had had a diamond set in her front tooth. The tooth was recovered from the uncle, the diamond sold and the proceeds given to the children.

Every charities district is supposed to have men and women in it who keep in touch with the cases in their district. But life in the modern city is so complicated and diversified, and there are so many demands upon the time of its citizens that the tendency is to get into a groove, to meet only the people who have the same interests and who do the same things as oneself. The average citizen never meets his foreign neighbors or knows anything of their lives. He looks upon them as an alien class with whom he has nothing in common. The United Charities is able, with its various branches of work, to put him in communication with large groups of people living near his own neighborhood.

I recall many cases where one was moved to pity. A family of eleven who slept in two rooms, the father a day laborer, ill with pneumonia, the mother slightly demented, three of the children feeble-minded. One of the rooms had no windows. This family were moved to better quarters, the house was reported to a sanitary inspector, two of the children placed in institutions, the father sent to a hospital and a pension given to the mother, together with instructions how to care for the children. That tuberculosis grows and thrives in homes like these is well known, and morning after morning, case after case came before my committee where the father or the mother had been obliged to give up work because of this disease. Fortunately the ravages of the disease are now much less since the establishment of the Municipal Tuberculosis Sanitarium, and the administrations of the tuberculosis nurses who not only suggest preventive measures, but are able to check the disease in its incipient stages.

One day I went to see an old woman of sixty. She lived on Walton Place only about a block from the Lake Shore Drive. For two or three years she had been existing upon the food she had procured from the garbage cans in the neighborhood and from the samples given her at the demonstration counters in the department stores. She took care of a child of a neighbor, for which she received fifty cents a week, and with this she paid the rent of a miserable room in the basement of an apartment house. When I visited her there was absolutely nothing in the room except one teacup and saucer, a cot and a coal shovel on which she warmed in the furnace of the building the food she found in the garbage boxes. Her only bed covering consisted of newspapers given her by the janitor in the build-

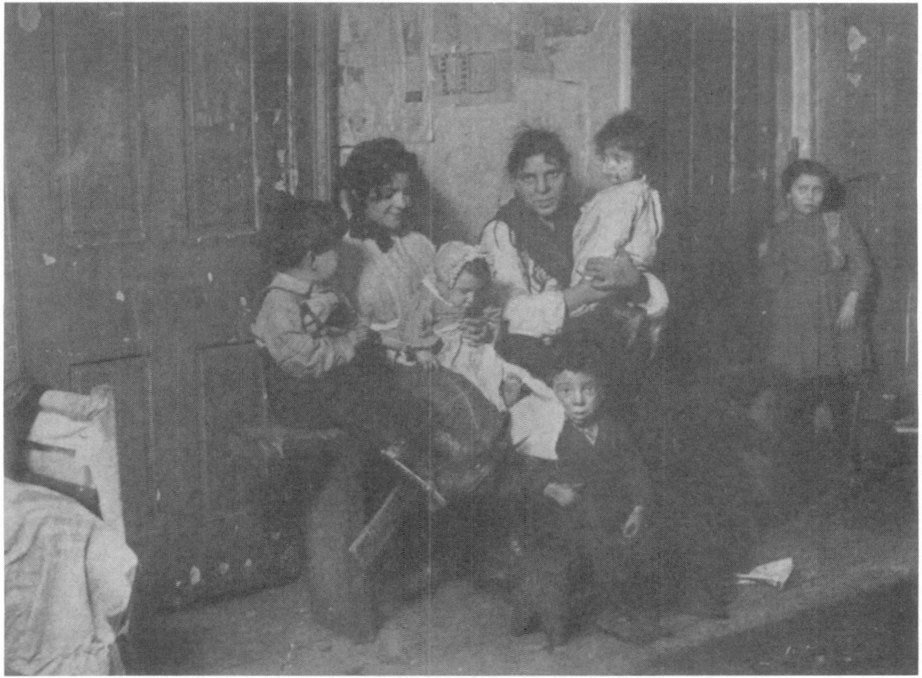

A TYPICAL UNITED CHARITIES FAMILY.

ing. Yet this woman came to Chicago from England with forty thousand dollars. A man to whom she entrusted the money for investment cheated her out of it. She was sent to a hospital where she died. In her last moments she tried to tell where she had hidden the money she had saved for her funeral expenses, but a search of her room revealed nothing, and she was buried by the Charities.

I had many ludicrous experiences with my committee because they felt at times that we were not doing the right thing. There was another old English woman who had seen better days. She had lost one leg and one eye. She lived in a wretched room infested with rats. She had no fire, and she wore upon her hands knitted gloves in order that her hands might be warm enough to hold her needles with which she tried to knit stockings. She had some stomach trouble and she subsisted entirely on beer which she had to take through a rubber tube. There was a temperance parson on the committee who didn't feel that the United Charities ought to spend its money on beer. In vain I represented to him that the poor woman in question could not get much enjoyment out of it since she had to take it through a rubber tube, but he was adamant, and said it was wicked. I finally quite frankly told him that I didn't care what he thought—that this woman was going to be supplied with beer as her only food just as long as I was chairman of that committee.

Another time when there was great unemployment, and we were beset with applicants for work, there came to us, among others, a young bank clerk who had always done indoor work, and who apparently had a tendency toward tuberculosis. About this time there was a heavy snowfall, and we could get plenty of jobs for men who were willing to shovel snow. A well known clergyman on the committee insisted that this young bank clerk be set to do this heavy work. I remonstrated, but finally yielded. The man manfully took the work, promptly caught cold, and died of pneumonia.

It was very difficult to get people to follow a line of conduct prescribed for them by the United Charities. We once found a man begging on Chicago Avenue. He seemed to be very loose-jointed and had tied up his legs under him so skillfully that a glance at him would lead you to suppose he had lost his legs from the knees down. He made about ten dollars a day begging, and apparently led a very enjoyable life. By entreating him to "Stand up and be a man," and by threatening that we would cause his arrest if he did not, we finally persuaded him to let down his legs and go to work. Unfortunately, parts of our anatomy which receive no use, naturally become useless in time, and the man, much to his astonishment, found he could not use his legs, not even stand on them. He was so genuinely distressed that we sent him to a hospital where he remained three months, having his legs massaged and receiving all kinds of treatment calculated to restore them to normality. At the end of three months he was reported cured, we then secured a place for him in a store where he could sit most of the time and where his duties were light, and we contemplated, with some pleasure, our handiwork. Alas! Two days later our investigator found him with his legs again tied up under him, in the identical place on Chicago Avenue where she had first seen him. He said begging was much easier than doing any work, and he liked it much better.

This story reminds me that while it is easy to sketch out a plan of action for an individual, it is often difficult to make the person adhere to the plan.

I remember one very pretty girl who had been leading a disreputable life, we tried to persuade her to give it up and thought we had been successful. She left the house where she had been living and we found her a place in a factory where she had fairly light work. At the end of a week she came to tell me that she had left the factory and gone back to her previous occupation. She said, "It is easy enough for you with your fine clothes and your soft food, to preach to a girl like me, but I just cannot stand working all day and going home at night to a miserable little hall bedroom where I cannot even see to read, and I am going back where at least I will have some comfort and companionship."

We felt at one time that we must give some kind

of an object lesson in regard to eating food which had not been prepared in a cleanly manner and which was contaminated in consequence. There was an Industrial Exhibition given about this time by the Consumers League, showing sweat shop labor, and we moved one of our tubercular families down to the exhibition; they were shown in a room which was squalid and dirty, the mother, father, two girls and a boy had tuberculosis, the mother and father in the last stages, coughing constantly. On the bed, the chairs and tables were dishes of nuts, as the family subsisted on the pay which they earned by shelling these nuts, and they worked diligently during the exhibition. Down near the front of the booth, was a large pan of shelled nuts and on it was a sign saying "These nuts were all shelled by a family who have tuberculosis." It was a great surprise to us to see everyone who passed this booth, look at the family with great interest, carefully read the sign and then help themselves to the nuts which they ate with great fervor. We were disgusted at our attempt to visualize the dangers of tuberculosis, and we had many doubts whether it was at all ethical to have asked this family to do their work and parade their illness in such a public place.

This reminds me of relief-giving in the early days by the churches, when every family sent in a turkey for distribution and when every recipient grabbed just as many turkeys as possible. I remember an old blind couple who went to my church, who showed me with great pride the five turkeys they had managed to get from the church for their Christmas dinner. And this recalls a later experience at Hull-House: One of the newspapers here had asked if Hull-House would distribute some of their Christmas baskets for them. We said we would be glad to do so, but we needed four hundred for the poor of the neighborhood. The reply was that they would be sent to us two days before Christmas. They did not arrive. We telephoned but were told they were on their way. On the day before Christmas they were still apparently on their way. The women who came to get them at the House gathered in the parlors, waiting anxiously. Noon came; no baskets! Six o'clock; no baskets! And finally, when Miss Addams telephoned again the newspaper said they had given them all away. Miss Addams telephoned me to know if I could suggest anything. "There were four hundred people waiting downstairs. She couldn't bear to disappoint them." I said, "Give them each two or three dollars." She said, "We have no money." I told her I would see if I could get it. It was ten o'clock Christmas Eve. I got hold of the druggist in my neighborhood and asked his advice. He said there was an all-night bank open in his neighborhood; he would take me there and introduce me. I went, gave my check and drew out some money, but unfortunately it was only in one-hundred dollar bills. They had no small ones. I then telephoned to the president of my own bank and told him my trouble. He said, "Those poor people shall have their money tonight." He telephoned a clerk, got him out of bed, sent him down to the bank and several hundred dollars was given me in one dollar bills. We got over to Hull-House about midnight, and the four hundred people who were waiting went home happy, because they could purchase a Christmas dinner at one of their neighborhood stores the following morning.

All these experiences with help-giving agencies and with the poor people of my neighborhood were most illuminating, as well as interesting, and we could not but feel that the advent of these foreign people who had come among us was a stirring call to some form of social service which probably would demand personal sacrifice. The question has always been, how to get it.

I was elected the vice president of the United Charities after having served about twelve years on the advisory committee, but I must confess that being a vice president, often presiding at meetings of the board and being occupied with larger questions, such as the making out of the budget, the question of raising money, etc., may be very necessary, but it is not by any means as interesting as the actual contact with the people who need help. Two or three years ago I visited in my capacity as vice president, all of the district offices of the United Charities, talking with the superintendents, making suggestions for betterment, and trying to standardize the work of all the districts. This was perhaps getting a little bit nearer to the neighborhood, but on the whole did not compare for interest with my work as chairman of the Lower North District.

Fortunately, the activities of the United Charities and other organizations, the administration of the Mothers' Pension Act, the Workmen's Compensation Law, and the practical cessation of immigration, have had a tendency to reduce the quantity of destitution in Chicago and prevent family breakdowns; we, therefore, seldom find now the terrible conditions which horrified me twenty years ago. Even the number of families applying to the United Charities is less. In 1916 there were 14,670, in 1925 12,022.

The specialized agencies, such as the Infant Welfare Society, the Visiting Nurse Association, etc., and the commitment of the insane and the feebleminded to institutions has taught people to take better care of themselves through preventive measures, and illness and accident in the families of the United Charities have decreased, in the period from 1916 to 1925, from 74% to 50%.

Strange as it may seem, and in spite of the prevalence of divorce, desertion (the poor man's divorce) has decreased, during the above period, from 7% to 4%.

Owing to the efforts of the tuberculosis nurses, and others, to stamp out tuberculosis, and the establishment of the Municipal Tuberculosis Sanitarium, this dread disease is no longer feared as in the past, and has decreased, from 1916 to 1925, from 12% to 2% of United Charities cases.

During the first few years after the Volstead Act was enforced, drinking was much less among the families of the United Charities. Unfortunately, within the last three years, intemperance has increased 100% a year and, although it is not as high as it was before prohibition, it is rapidly mounting.

Altogether, the United Charities has every reason to be encouraged at its success in preventing family breakdowns, and in its efforts toward preventive poverty and family rehabilitation. It has now ten district offices, 133 employees and an annual budget of $623,000. It is a huge machine for family reconstruction, but, unlike most machines, it has a heart, and its kindly trained executives regard any applicant for help as a human being. By their efficacy of effort and their sympathy and encouragement they rebuild this human being and his family so that he and they may have a chance for health, for education, for work, for the decencies of life and for happiness.

CHAPTER V

HULL-HOUSE

All through this earlier part of my life my attention had been turned toward the lack of adequate housing for people of a great city, and I felt most strongly that better homes were the most necessary things in the world. About this time I had heard vaguely of Hull-House and of its founder, Jane Addams. My curiosity was greatly aroused by what I had heard of her, a young girl, rather delicate, very well educated, who had traveled a great deal, but who had such a sympathy for her fellowmen that she had established herself, with a friend, Miss Ellen Starr, in an old house belonging to the Hull family, and which had been given her, rent free, by Miss Helen Culver, its owner. This house was situated at the corner of Halsted and Polk Streets.

About this time I had a young friend who was tired of social life, and who was anxious to do something worth while. She asked my advice about going to live at Hull-House, and finally established herself there for the winter; meantime, I had heard Jane Addams speak at a meeting concerning the great strike at the Pullman Company; I remember she likened Mr. Pullman to King Lear, and she seemed so fair and so dispassionate in her setting forth the reason of this strike and her feeling that Mr. Pullman had wanted to do everything for his employees but that he wanted to do it in his own way, that I was much impressed by her sympathy for the working man, and the sense of justice which made her see Mr. Pullman's side. Soon after I went over to Hull-House to visit my friend, and I was much interested in some stories which she told me of her work in the neighborhood, and I remember giving some money to be used for the poor, the first donation I had ever made to Hull-House. I then met Miss Addams, and she asked me if I would come over there and do some work; when I asked what kind, she said she wished I would join the Hull-House Woman's Club, composed of the women of the neighborhood, which had recently been formed. When I asked what I should do, Miss Addams suggested that I lead the women in making motions and in helping them to think on the subjects which came before them, and in helping them express their thoughts. This all seemed to me rather vague, and I was rather frightened at the prospect; I knew almost nothing of parliamentary law, but immediately joined a class on the North Side with a good teacher and about ten women as members. I studied very hard, had a great many meetings and finally felt that at least I knew the parliamentary ropes. I then joined the Hull-House Woman's Club, and when a question came up for discussion I usually made the motion and talked to it, and the women were quick to learn and to follow. Some time later I was made secretary of this club and still later was elected President. For about seventeen years I filled some official position in the club, many years being president, and I have always felt that any experience I acquired in speaking was entirely due to practice in this club. I can see the crowded room now, filled with tired women, a few of them with shawls over their heads, some of them with babies in their arms or clinging to their skirts; there was always a good deal of noise, the women were restless, the air was heavy and stuffy, but no one wanted a window open. On the front row sat the eldest members of the club, most of them wore little black bonnets with ribbons tied under their chins. They had an invariable habit of going to sleep, and when I was speaking and saw them begin to nod it always acted as a tonic because I brightened up and tried to be so entertaining or startling in my remarks that they would come to with a jerk, and the test of my speaking was—could I keep that front bench looking intelligent and awake?

I have many funny recollections of this club. One day a Christian Scientist came to speak to us; she made a most lengthy address, and at the end said, "Now here in this neighborhood, when you are out at night, just as the sun is setting and you go down to the river and notice the odors which arise from it, you must think of the pine trees and how they smell and say to yourself, 'Oh! what a lovely evening; how sweet everything smells!' " One old German woman arose and said, "Vell, all I can say is if dot woman say that river smell good then there must be something the matter with dot woman's nose." There was a perfect roar from the club, and many a nod of assent, for the Chicago River, at that time, was a black slimy stream, and most unattractive in every way.

This Hull-House Woman's Club was most successful as a club, and rapidly increased in numbers until it overflowed the room in which it had started; it then moved into the big theatre connected with Hull-House and when it had crowded that theatre to capacity, I built a hall especially for it which was later named "Bowen Hall." This building has a beautiful auditorium seating 800 people; a club library was established which provided light literature for the members, and the club not only interested itself in all the welfare projects of the city but it made many garments for the poor. It had a Sunshine Fund for its own sick members, and it became a really important club. Its membership increased to nearly a thousand; it held meetings once a week and once a year my husband and I gave a ball to the club members and their husbands. It was not a case of invitations where you may count upon one-third of the invited accepting, it was a case of every person who was invited coming if she was able. They not only came, but they brought their husbands, their children, and often guests. The ball was run in three divisions, a dance in Bowen Hall, moving pictures in the gymnasium, a large and sustantial supper in the coffee house. Tickets of different colors admitted the guests to the different buildings, when one entertainment was over in one place, the guests changed to another, those in Bowen Hall going to the gymnasium, those in the gymnasium going to supper; the three sets did not meet until the very last, when they all came into Bowen Hall to say good-bye. These balls were most popular with the club members and Mr. Bowen and I enjoyed them just as much, but were so tired, after shaking hands with something like 2400 people, leading the grand march and making speeches of welcome, that we were almost ill.

I often felt at this Hull-House club that not even in church did I ever get the inspiration or the desire for service, so much as when I was presiding at a meeting of the club and sat on the platform and looked down on the faces of 800 or 900 women gathered together, all intensely in earnest and all most anxious perhaps to put over some project in which they were interested. The club also proved to be a liberal education for me. At our weekly meetings we always had a speaker for the day. Speakers were not then always trustworthy, sometimes they failed to appear and I was so afraid that we would be without an entertainment that I made it a point to post myself every week on the topic of the day and have something ready to say on the subject announced. This gave me a wide insight into matters of the day and, incidentally, much information and instruction on many questions in literature, science and practical matters.

My first speeches were made at Hull-House. I never had spoken before and felt very nervous when I got on my feet; I found it difficult to collect my thoughts. It was, however, good practice to do it amidst so much confusion; frequently when I was speaking, the door of the room would be thrown open and some of the residents (who were doing what they called "toting"—that is, showing people around Hull-House) would say, "This is the Hull-House Woman's Club, that is Mrs. Bowen, the president, on the platform," and it was very difficult not to listen to the comments of the visitors, as I was trying to put my own thoughts in order. From that time on I spoke a great deal and for many winters averaged about five speeches a week. My experiences in the Juvenile Protective Association always supplied me with ample material.

About this time I was made a trustee and the treasurer of Hull-House Association and I was very proud to be one of the trustees who formed a self-perpetuating body. During this time I had seen a great deal of Miss Addams; I admired her greatly and loved her dearly. She impressed me then as always being very sad, as if the sorrows of the neighborhood were pressing upon her, which indeed they were. She was the receptacle into which all the troubles of the district were poured; she was expected to give help and sympathy and financial aid and all kinds of advice. She was having hard work financing Hull-House. Many people felt she was too much in sympathy with the laboring people and some business men listened to exaggerated tales of what they heard went on at the House and refused to help, but there were others who, because of their contact with the House and of their knowledge of the unselfish and devoted work which was done by the residents and especially by Miss Addams, felt that there was nothing else in the city which was such a power for good, not only to the people of the neighborhood but to the whole community.

I had to go to Miss Addams very often with things pertaining to the club; I wanted to know, as did all the other neighbors, what to do under certain circumstances. There were many times when I was puzzled and entirely at sea. Miss Addams always had a very clear vision and a great sense of justice and I can remember my mortification one day, when I said, "I have done everything in the world for that woman and she is not even grateful." She looked at me quizzically and said, "Is that the reason you helped her, because you wanted gratitude?" She was, however, never condemning but always reassuring and encouraging. I can remember the first speech I ever made, how much she helped me with it, how kindly was her comment on what I had said.

Miss Addams had a rare way of putting people in a position of responsibility and then letting them work out their own plans; she always commended them for what they had done although, in a very wise way she managed to let them see the imperfections of their plan and how much it might be bettered another time. She had a marvelous influence over the people who went to Hull-House, she could almost always make anyone get up and speak. I remember early in my connection with the House I was in a big meeting and after Miss Addams had spoken, she looked over the audience and said, "Mrs. Bowen will now continue this subject." It was one about which I knew something but had never spoken on, still I never thought of refusing and therefore gained confidence which has never left me.

I have never seen Miss Addams floored on being asked to speak on any subject. One day when I was sitting next to her she was called to the platform to speak on the subject of music, and I thought, now they have her, I do not believe she can speak on that subject, but she did and spoke most beautifully.

There were at this time about nine thousand people coming every week to Hull-House for clubs or classes, performances in the theatre, dances in one of the halls, or for advice or assistance. Miss Addams saw a large part of these people. She listened to their stories, gave them good advice, and helped them whenever possible. The neighbors came to her with all kinds of troubles. I remember being over there one night when a request came for her to go and see a little Italian boy who was dying. She took me with her. It was a dark night and pouring rain. We went up some very narrow streets with no lights on them. Stopping before a squalid looking house, up two flights of stairs, through unlighted halls, we finally came into a small room, crowded with weeping Italians, and on the bed there lay a little boy of eight or ten years, who wanted to say good-bye to Miss Addams. She was so sympathetic with the people and so tender to the little boy that I came away with a new impression of what she meant to all the people whose lives touched hers so frequently.

Hull-House was a great power in the city. Miss Addams had most progressive ideas of what should be done to make a city safe for its young people. Hull-House had the first public play ground, which it maintained for some time before it was taken over by the city. Many reforms were instituted by Hull-House. One of its residents was made inspector of garbage in her district. Another resident became a factory inspector. Some of the trained nurses in the neighborhood lived at the House.

Many a meeting have I attended there of protest against what was being done by the city or county authorities. Many a remonstrance went from the House against the evils which constantly spring up in every great city. Since that time play grounds have been established and community centers erected, vacation schools have been opened, play ground associations have taken charge of vacant lots, but there was a time when almost all of these activities emanated in a measure from Hull-House Association, and from the brain of its founder, Jane Addams.

We were all very much interested in the boy question, and feeling that in that neighborhood there was very little in the way of recreation, Miss Addams and I were most anxious for a boys' club house. Together we visited boys' clubs in New York and in other places, and finally I was able to erect a large, five-story building adjoining Hull-House, which has always been known as the Boys' Club. About twenty-five hundred boys immediately became members of it. Its first floor had bowling alleys and shops for blacksmithing, carpentry, electrical construction, cobbling and the making of pottery. Its second floor had billiard and pool rooms, a large room for the band, and the rest of the building contained quarters for the people who were in charge, together with library, study room, etc. Miss Helen Culver gave an endowment for the building which then was a sufficient sum to cover its expenses, but since then more money has been needed. The opening of this club attracted a great deal of attention, and people came from all over the city and from different parts of the country to see it. In my presentation of the building I said that "Boys' clubs were better than policemen's clubs," and this was really the keynote of what we were trying to do; namely, give boys proper recreation, and not allow them to get their amusements amid the dirt of the streets.

Later on, I gave as a memorial for my husband to Hull-House Association seventy-two acres of ground at Waukegan, Illinois. These grounds have on them ravines, beautiful trees, flower and vegetable gardens, a play-ground, a swimming pool, a recreation hall, a large commons where all the children eat and something like eight other buildings which house the children who go there. The place has sleeping accommodations for 225 people and the children go up for two weeks at a time. There is a trained nurse on hand and the health of the children is most carefully guarded. I called the place the Joseph T. Bowen Country Club, as I wanted the guests of the club to feel, not that it was a charity in any way, but that it was a club of their own. The place was dedicated out under the trees on a beautiful June afternoon, and I have never gotten as much pleasure out of anything as I have in visiting this club and in seeing the boys' and girls' enjoyment when they first arrive there.

The club is endowed, but Hull-House raises the money every summer for the food for the children, the endowment simply paying for the up-keep of the place and buildings and the salaries of the gardeners who keep it in order. Several buildings were erected on the grounds by people interested in the club, but it is run by Hull-House Association.

Miss Addams spoke at the opening of this club and if anything could give comfort to one who, after twenty-five years of being happily married, had lost the person nearest and dearest to her, it came to me at that time, for she spoke so sympathetically and so appreciatively of my husband.

Miss Addams is a deeply religious woman; I do not think she shows it by church going but she does manifest it by following the footsteps of the Founder of the Christian Religion. Even during the war when, following her Quaker teachings, she declared herself a pacifist, she endured a perfect martyrdom because of the storm of disapproval directed against her. She never resented the manner in which she was sometimes treated and often misrepresented, but continued her efforts to bring about peace, with a courage which even her adversaries could not but admire.

My whole acquaintance with Hull-House opened for me a new door into life. I met many prominent people there, because anyone who came to Chicago always wanted to visit the House. I have dined there with many celebrities, and always found it

THE PLAYGROUND AT THE BOWEN COUNTRY CLUB.

most interesting, and on the other hand I have made many good friends among working people and have come in contact with problems and situations about which I would have otherwise known nothing.

Miss Addams in these early days was really an interpreter between working men and women and the people who lived in luxury on the other side of the city and she also gave the people of her own neighborhood quite a different idea about the men and women who were ordinarily called "capitalists."

To come in contact constantly with the people of that neighborhood certainly gave one a new impression of life in a great city, and I began to feel that what was needed more than anything was an acquaintance between the well-to-do and those less well off. Until an acquaintance of this kind can be effected, there will always be difficulties and there never will be that sympathy which should exist.

In the Hull-House Woman's Club I tried to get more close to the members by having every Wednesday at Hull-House a luncheon of twenty-five members of the club, and I began at the beginning until every member had been invited, and then began all over again. We sat at one very large table in the residents' dining-room. We had only one rule, which was that only one person was to speak at a time. I have often wished that the same rule could prevail at many luncheon parties I have attended. To be sure, I usually started the conversation with some topic of the day in which I was interested, and then the other women would speak, one by one, and give their opinions. Sometimes rather funny things occurred. I remember one woman asking to speak, and suddenly saying, "Pardon me, but Hull-House is cheating you on this coffee, because it is awfully poor!"

Often Hull-House women came to me for help. I shall never forget one of the nicest women in the club who was in a terrible situation. She had had a telegram that her sister had been suddenly killed in an automobile accident in another town and she was to come down and get the body. She had no money in the house, but she was treasurer of a benefit society and in the excitement of the moment, feeling that she must have money, she took $100 from the treasury and went after the sister, believing that she could repay it, because "she had a rich cousin who she knew would help her." She got the sister's body, brought her back and buried her, and then went to the rich cousin, who refused to give her a cent, and the poor woman found herself in the position of having looted the treasury of her society. There were many pathetic cases of this kind, for, in a big settlement club, such as the one I have been describing, one cuts through a cross section of human beings, as it were, and it was most interesting to realize that although the people I met at Hull-House lived a life far removed from the kind I led, yet, after all we are all cast in the same mold, all with the same emotions, the same feelings, the same sense of right and wrong, but, alas, not with the same opportunities.

I made many speeches at this time on all kinds of subjects from the "Fertilization of Flowers" to "Traveling in Foreign Countries." I had taken photographs in Egypt, Greece, Turkey, France, Italy and Mexico and when I returned to this country I had these photographs made into slides and wrote lectures to accompany them. I gave these different lectures for several years, before many of the clubs in the city and as they depicted experiences of my own, street scenes and matters of this kind, they always seemed to be popular. I remember giving a series of them at Bowen Hall, Hull-House, on Sunday evenings one winter, with the hall, crowded with people who came in from the neighborhood and who loved the warmth and sense of cheer and entertainment provided. This reminds me how often I have seen Bowen Hall filled with a crowd of this kind. One winter, when there was a great deal of unemployment, it was opened every Sunday afternoon and was crowded with the unemployed. Miss Addams and I always spoke to the men, trying to encourage them, telling them to hold on and not give up. We always provided a large roast beef sandwich and hot coffee, and many Sunday afternoons I was so tired I could hardly stand up after having been on my feet passing these refreshments, but I was much pleased one day to have a man tell me that he had been going to commit suicide but what I had said to him the previous Sunday had kept him from it.

After these meetings were over I was told one day that a man wanted to see me. He was a very ordinary looking person whom I recognized as one of the leaders of the men who were out of work. He said he had come to see me to express the gratitude of the men for what I had done for them that winter and that they had clubbed together to give me a present. He knew it was a very poor one but it was all they could afford and he hoped I would enjoy it; with that he handed me a dirty little brown package with one pound of dates in it. I thanked him and accepted the package, feeling very much touched by this evidence of good will.

One winter many years ago, there was a strike of the garment workers in Chicago. It was a long and bitter fight, neither side would give in or compromise. The workers were not as well organized as now and received very little in the way of strike benefits. Reports were frequently brought to us at Hull-House, of children who were suffering for food. We formed a committee and I raised about $12,000, and made arrangements with milkmen to deliver milk at certain stations throughout the city, and here the strikers obtained it, without charge, for their babies. I made many speeches at this time to raise this money, not taking either side in the controversy but feeling that the children were non-combatants and were entitled to have food enough on which to sustain life. I remember one most successful meeting just before Christmas when I spoke of the babies who were dying, as the "Slaughter of the Innocents," and I begged the women who were in the audience to give me the money for milk which they would otherwise spend for presents for their children. Woman after woman came forward and literally emptied her purse into a hat which I had placed on the table. I forget how much was received but it was a large sum.

Christmas Eve was always very exciting at Hull-House. The residents trimmed tiny Christmas trees with candles and with many little gifts which they had specially prepared for the children. The preparations for Christmas absorbed a great deal of attention. For days beforehand we worked in one of the big rooms where there were barrels of turkeys, sweet potatoes, cranberries, apples and oranges. Sometimes as many as four hundred baskets were made up from the contents of these barrels. Several hundred pounds of candy was purchased and this was put into boxes and distributed to the children as they came to the various Christmas festivities.

The Music School had always a most charming entertainment in Bowen Hall on the Sunday preceding Christmas. The hall would be filled to overflowing, on the stage were the children of the

Music School: they sang Christmas carols and, on a platform just over their heads, was shown in a series of most beautiful tableaux, the Annunciation, the Manger, the Shepherds, the Visit of the Magi, and so on. It was always a thrilling moment to sit in this crowded hall, to hear the children's tender little voices rise high in the Christmas music and to see those beautiful tableaux which portrayed the Birth of Christ. It was impossible to look at these pictures and to listen to the music without being dominated by the Christmas spirit which fairly radiated through the hall. This event was always followed by a huge Christmas tree for the children, the tree covered with white, its branches nearly touching the top of the vaulted ceiling of the coffee house, seemed to embody the freshness and purity of the forest.

On New Year's Day the Woman's Club always had Bowen Hall filled with its members, their husbands and all their relatives, and we came together to hear stories told by the old settlers of Chicago. As these old ladies and gentlemen grew older they became more rambling and incoherent in their talk so that occasionally we had to lead them from the platform to keep them from going on forever. In time these Old Settlers' meetings were given up because most of the old settlers died.

The one person all the neighborhood wanted to here was Miss Addams and as she would stand up to speak you could fairly feel the love which radiated toward her from every person in the audience.

Bowen Hall has been used for all kinds of meetings. The Hull-House band gave concerts there and perhaps one of the hardest things I ever had to do was to sit on the platform while the band of seventy pieces played a few feet away from me and nearly demolished my ear drums, although Colonel Roosevelt, who was the guest of honor on this occasion, insisted that they should play again. I remember one pathetic meeting after the war when the place was filled with soldiers who had returned, most of whom had gone from Hull-House. They were all disheartened and disillusioned, they could not find work, some of them did not want to work, saying they were tired. Miss Addams and I tried to cheer them up and to restore to them something of the spirit which they seemed to have lost in the war. During this period of unemployment, we raised quite a large sum of money at Hull-House and engaged men to work around the House and at the Country Club at Waukegan. The men were put under a good superintendent and they swept and cleaned, washed walls and painted all the buildings, repaired clocks and violins, mended and pressed clothing, cobbled shoes and were then paid for their services. I remember one young man who had been a tight-rope walker in a circus; for a long time we could not think of anything he was trained to do but after a time we set him to washing windows and never was there such a window washer; balancing himself on a window sill far up from the street he would wash most assiduously and apparently enjoy his work. One could not but feel sorry for some of the men and the kind of work they had to do. There was one poet and the only job available for him was to run a vacuum cleaner, a piece of work for which he was grateful, but one which was not congenial. It was, however, a great surprise and a gratification to find that these men who were out of work not only were willing to adapt themselves to occupations they had never before attempted, but that they did it willingly and cheerfully, with never a complaint concerning the unfamiliarity of the work. It certainly was a lesson to me to be patient when I did not always get what I wanted.

One day, one of the physicians who lived at Hull-House made an impassioned appeal for help for a poor family before the Hull-House Club. Going up to her afterwards, I emptied my purse and said, "I am sorry there is only two dollars in it but you can have it all." She looked at me and said, "My good woman, do you think you can afford so much?" I immediately said "Yes." She still did not want to accept it and said, "Do you not think you should ask your husband before you give so large a gift?" I said I would tell him but I was sure he would not mind. I was greatly pleased at the time because I thought it showed I had accomplished my object of being just one of the members of the club.

For many years I went to these club meetings, driving in a buggy and wearing my most simple clothes, but afterwards I found this was a mistake, the women wanted good clothes, they liked to see me dressed smartly, they liked to have me drive up in a motor and to see it standing in front of the club house on Polk Street. I always told my friends that I had to keep up a certain number of social activities in order to get my name in the papers to please the Hull-House Woman's Club. Many a time they would say, "We saw your name in the paper as being at the opera." "We were glad to know our club president was at a ball." "It is a pleasure to know we have for president a lady who goes so much into society." On one occasion a reporter almost ruined me. He wanted to take my picture showing me as a society woman befriending a child at Hull-House, so he took my photograph one day when I had my arm over the shoulder of a little boy. Unfortunately the photographer did not think I was dressed (or undressed) enough to represent a society woman; he therefore took off my head and put it on the body of a very slim woman who was very decollete and who showed much more of her person than I was in the habit of doing; as a result, the Hull-House Club said they "were disappointed in me." "They did not think I would ever wear such a low dress," etc., and I had almost to make a public announcement that the body and clothes belonged to another woman.

I gave up the presidency of the Hull-House Club because at that time I was made president of the Woman's City Club and it seemed to me only just and wise to give up this settlement club in which I had been so happy, to someone else and to begin what perhaps was a larger piece of work.

As I look back over the years I have been connected with Hull-House and its many activities, I feel that, in a certain measure, I received there from Miss Addams the training and education in social work which is now given at the Schools of Civics and Philanthropy. My instruction, however, did not come from text books or lectures, but from Miss Addams' teaching and from my personal experience with the many people with whom I came in contact. For this teaching and for this experience, I have been always grateful.

CHAPTER VI

THE JUVENILE COURT*

My first knowledge of the Juvenile Court came through Mrs. James M. Flower, to whose vision and love for children that court owes so much. Mrs. Flower soon demonstrated to me the great need of a court where children should not be treated as criminals, but as delinquent children needing wise direction, care and correction, and also the need of a place where they could be confined, awaiting their hearing in the court. She told me of many pitiful cases of little children confined in the police stations or jails and of one boy who had been bitten by rats in one of the latter. It was, I think, about this time that my imagination was caught by a cartoon; the first part represented a steep precipice over which little children were constantly falling. At the bottom stood a long row of ambulances to take the injured to the hospital but no attempt was made to keep the children from the

*The following chapter on the Juvenile Court was first made as a speech at the commemoration of the twenty-fifth Anniversary of the Juvenile Court. It was printed in a book called "The Child, The Clinic and The Court," published in 1925 by the New Republic, Inc., in coöperation with the Wieboldt Foundation.

edge of the precipice. The second part showed how the Juvenile Court formed a fence at the top of the precipice and the children were prevented from falling over. At any rate, that cartoon (ahead of its time) described very well the effort of the Juvenile Court to save children, and since then the court has made a continuous effort to educate parents to raise the standards of the home, and to keep children from committing the various crimes and misdemeanors which take them into the court.

Mrs. Flower at this time formed a Committee of citizens called the Juvenile Court Committee; Miss Julia Lathrop was its first president. I succeeded her I think in 1900. The law provided for the establishment of a court and for the services of probation officers, but it made no provision for the salary of these officers nor did it provide for a place of detention, although it specifically set forth that children were not to be confined in jails or police stations.

The Juvenile Court Committee then raised the money for the salaries of the probation officers, beginning with five and ending with twenty-two. It called an educator of note, Mr. Henry W. Thurston, to be chief probation officer; it also paid an assistant chief probation officer and the salaries of one or two clerks in the court. During this time the probation officers were most carefully selected by the Juvenile Court Committee; they met frequently with the members of the committee at Hull-House and we talked over their duties with them. We really knew absolutely nothing about these subjects; there was no literature on Juvenile Courts at that time, or on the work of probation officers and those of us who had the training of these officers had to fall back on our own knowledge of human nature and on our best guess as to their duties.

We felt that a civil service examination was the only proper method of securing these officers and we conducted such examinations as best we knew how.

I think our first probation officer was Mrs. Alzina Stevens, perhaps the best example of what a probation officer should be. Her great desire was to be of use to her fellow men. Her love of children was great; her singleness of purpose and strength of character so remarkable that she exerted a great influence over the children committed to her charge. I find among some of my old papers the following which I wrote concerning the duties of probation officers: "They must be men and women of many sides, endowed with the strength of a Samson and the delicacy of an Ariel. They must be tactful, skilful, firm and patient. They must know how to proceed with wisdom and intelligence and must be endowed with that rare virtue, common sense." These qualities would seem to be needed just as much today as they were twenty-five years ago.

At this time we had no place to confine children pending their hearing. They could not be kept in the jails or the police stations so we took an old house on West Adams Street which had been fitted up as a detention home and run by the Illinois Industrial Association. They could not support it so it was taken over by the Juvenile Court Committee. The girls and the dependent children were kept in the house, which was a very simple, homelike place. Behind it was a large, two-story building which had been used as a stable. We fitted this up, using the first floor as a kitchen and sitting room and the second floor as sleeping quarters. It contained fifty beds for the boys who were confined there. We maintained this house for seven years in cooperation with the city and county, from twenty-six to twenty-eight hundred children passing through it yearly. The city allowed us eleven cents a day for food for each child and the county gave us certain things, among others the services of the county physician, transportation to and from the court, etc. During these seven years the institution was never quarantined on account of contagious diseases. When a child was ill the county physician was immediately called and if the child had a contagious disease he was at once removed to, I think, the contagious ward in the county hospital.

We had at that time a fine body of men and women who were most anxious for the success of the court and for the good of the children, and we finally secured the passage of a law which provided that probation officers be placed on the payroll of the county. I well remember how that law was passed because it gave me a feeling of great uneasiness. I happened to know at that time a noted Illinois politician; I asked him to my house and told him I wanted to get this law passed at once. The legislature was in session; he went to the telephone in my library, called up one of the bosses in the Senate and one in the House and said to each one, "There is a bill, number so and so, which I want passed; see that it is done at once." One of the men whom he called evidently said, "What is there in it?" and the reply was, "There is nothing in it, but a woman I know wants it passed." And it was passed. I thought with horror at the time, supposing it had been a bad bill, it would have been passed in exactly the same way.

The Juvenile Court Committee was at that time made up of women delegates from the various clubs. These clubs took a great interest in the Home; they visited it frequently, they pulled down the covers of the beds to see if they were clean, they tasted the food to see if it was good. Seldom a day passed without a visitor from one of these organizations and it certainly tended to keep us alert and active on the job. I remember at one time we were summoned into court charged with having served worms to the children in their soup; when we responded to the summons and listened to the evidence, it was found that one of the parents of the children had seen vermicelli in the soup and thought it was worms. Another time we were berated by a club because we only had one sheet on the beds. It was difficult for us to get the boys even to undress or to take off their shoes. They would strip the clean sheets off the bed, saying they could not bear to get them dirty, and one of their favorite tricks (smoking was not allowed) was to take the shoe strings out of their shoes to bed with them and smoke them in comfort until the guard for those fifty boys smelt the burning strings and hastened to confiscate them. We had a teacher from the Board of Education who was excellent with the boys and kept them occupied—the great secret of keeping boys out of mischief. She was very proud of her class and the boys themselves were proud of their progress.

Out in the back yard, between the house and the stable, was a little house which looked like a dog kennel; it really was a hand made fumigating outfit and the children's clothing was fumigated in it.

I suppose boys were very much then as they are now and yet we had almost no trouble with them. Our superintendent was a little old woman, I should say over seventy years of age, but there was nothing about children she did not know. On one occasion when I was at the Home she came in from the stable quite irate at the boys as they had been acting badly; I asked her what they were doing; she said, "Oh, I thought something was wrong and went out there and found they had the new guard (furnished by the city) on the floor bound and they were all sitting on him, jabbing his head with his own revolver." When I asked her if she called the police, she said, "No, indeed, why should I call the police? I told them to get up and unbind the guard and apologize at once." "Did they do it?" I asked, and she replied, "Why of course." That, as far as I remember, was the only outbreak we ever had.

On one occasion one of our best boys escaped from the Home. We were rather unhappy about it because we had given him certain privileges and he seemed a trustworthy boy. He returned at the end of the day very triumphant, carrying in each hand several chickens tied by the legs, and he said, "I felt so sorry for you ladies, you seemed to have such a hard time raising money to feed us kids that I just went out to Mrs. Story's chicken yard and got these chickens for you." He was very much upset and we felt almost apologetic to take the chickens away from him and return them to the rightful owner.

It was very difficult to get the city or the county authorities to give us any money or necessary equipment for the Home. The county had given us an old omnibus which was drawn by a very small horse who struggled painfully to drag the vehicle between the court and the Home. The old vehicle grew older and older and became very rickety and one day the driver came to say that some of the boards had fallen out of the bottom and he had nearly dropped the children on the street. The omnibus could not be repaired so I went to the county for relief and was told that this was a city matter and I must go to the Chief of Police. I went to his office and stood up against the wall all day; the office was full of expectorating gentlemen who occupied chairs and were rather amused at a woman waiting to see the Chief of Police. When I went to luncheon Miss Lathrop took my place in holding up the wall and we spun the day out that way until at dusk the Chief left by a back door. Next day I was in my place again and this time saw him. He said he had nothing to do with the matter and referred me to the repair department; they said the omnibus could not be repaired and referred me to the construction department; the construction department could do nothing about it unless it was ok'd by the Mayor, who referred us to the County Commissioners, who referred me to another department. After six weeks of seeing first one man and then another, in desperation the Juvenile Court Committee bought a new omnibus. It was too heavy for the little horse to pull so I went all over the ground again to get another horse. Finally, after having been referred to the Fire Department, I was informed there was a horse out on a farm that had been laid off because he was lame, but perhaps he could draw the omnibus. He was brought to the city and proved to be a large husky animal; he was harnessed to the omnibus with the little horse but evidently thought he was going to a fire and rushed down the street so rapidly that the driver had to stop him as the pony was nearly strangled from having been lifted off his feet.

We then bought a pair of horses and the city gave us a barn four miles from the Home. We were told several days later by the driver that the stalls in the barn were so small that the horses had not been able to lie down for four days and nights. Finding we could not do anything about the matter, we rented a stable for ourselves and tried to get the city to provide us with food for the horses. We even let them go three days without food, hoping in this way to force the city to provide for them. The whole thing ended in the committee buying its own omnibus, its own horses, renting its own stable and furnishing its own horse feed.

Some of the children who were brought into the Detention Home in these early days were pitiful objects. I remember two children, a boy and a girl, who had been found in a pig pen; their mother and father must have been insane because they had kept the children in with the animals, wearing no clothes and eating only the food furnished the pigs. They did not know how to talk and jabbered like little animals.

The early days of the court were without the services of a psychiatrist and we were not able to detect any dangerous tendencies on the part of the children. One day a sweet looking little boy, aged seven, with long curls down his back and a face like a cherub, took the kerosene can and when he was alone in the dormitory poured kerosene over all the beds and set fire to them. Be it said to the credit of all the other boys in the institution that they assisted in putting out the fire which, fortunately, did very little damage.

The Juvenile Court was held in one of the regular court rooms and two members of our committee always sat beside the judge to advise or assist in any way possible. The court room was always crowded, the air was heavy, there was almost no ventilation. Women of many nationalities filled the place, accompanied by stolid looking husbands, and many times they held babies in their arms. Many of the cases were most pitiful. I remember one twelve-year-old little girl held in her arms what I thought was a doll, and I later discovered to my horror that the "doll" was the child's own baby. She had forgotten the name of the father of the child. After a few years spent in this court room we felt that we must get the County Board to give us other quarters. We petitioned for rooms in the new county building on the top floor so that we might have plenty of air and light. What was called a "gentlemen's agreement" was made with the President of the County Board. The matter was, however, postponed from time to time, and we would then get different business men in the city to stop on their way to their offices and chat for a few moments with the president, asking him when he was going to set aside the use of a floor for the Juvenile Court. This was finally done, and the court housed in the county Building. The Juvenile Court soon outgrew these quarters and the Committee then tried to get the city and county to buy land and to erect a Juvenile Court Building with a Detention Home in connection with it. In this they were successful. The city furnished the land and the county appropriated $150,000 for the building. This structure on Ewing Street was used until the court moved into its present quarters about two years ago. During all these years the Juvenile Court Committee had kept in close touch not only with the probation officers and the Detention Home but with the judge of the Juvenile Court, and every year when a new judge to this court was to be appointed by the other Circuit Court judges, members of this committee saw all the judges and indicated the preference of the committee for some particular judge. In every instance, these judges appointed the men selected by the Juvenile Court Committee and as we look back over the judges who have served that court we feel very proud of them.

Judge Tuthill, the pioneer groping his way to find the right road, always kindly, always just, and with a sympathetic heart for the boy or girl who had gone wrong.

Judge Mack, who had given up most complicated and interesting legal work in order that he might help with the Children's Court. How ably he did it! We look back with the greatest pleasure and a thrill of pride not only to his decisions but to the educational campaign which he conducted at that time in order that the Juvenile Court might be interpreted to the people.

Then came Judge Pinckney, that kindly man who, in spite of real ill health, would not leave the court although ordered by his doctors to seek a field where there was not a constant demand upon his sympathies. His death may possibly be traced to his conscientious devotion to the court and to his disregard of repeated warnings. He was followed by Judge Arnold, the present incumbent, most eager and anxious to uphold the principles which had descended upon him from his illustrious predecessors.

The first woman judge in the Juvenile Court, Miss Mary M. Bartelme, who for years, without the honor of being a judge, was content to be his assistant and sat in the court working hard and conscientiously for the wards of the court. Not satisfied with ministering to them only through court procedure, she established homes for them and her warm love and sympathy follows them through all their lives. She has been a fine example for both men and women of what a judge should be and we are proud of her.

It is always a real satisfaction to know that politics has not yet dominated the Juvenile Court of Cook County; that we still have these judges who are incorruptible and devoted to their work.

In 1907 the Juvenile Court Committee, having raised and spent over $100,000, and having placed the Juvenile Court under the proper authorities, disbanded as the Juvenile Court Committee, but at the same time absorbed a small organization called the Juvenile Protective Association, started by Judge Mack, Mr. Hastings Hart and Miss Minnie Lowe. The Juvenile Court Committee changed the name to the Juvenile Protective Association and set about trying to keep children out of court by removing many of the demoralizing conditions which surrounded them. It is still at this work in the pool rooms, cabarets and dance halls, and many other places, trying to protect children and young people wherever they congregate.

When Judge Pinckney sat on the bench of the Juvenile Court he recognized that the appointment of probation officers was in his power. This was, of course, perfectly safe with him but many of us felt that it might not be wise to give a power of this kind to the judges of the future who might sit in the Juvenile Court, so Judge Pinckney appointed a committee of citizens, of which I had the honor to be chairman, to hold a civil service examination for probation officers. The committee was carefully chosen, as was the custom at that time, from Jews, Catholics and Protestants, an equal number of each. The committee found that so many people wanted to take the examination that it would have to be held in a large building; the Board of Education gave us a large high school and the examination was held on a Saturday. At a previous meeting each member of the Committee had brought in his or her own questions and on the day of the examination the whole committee met at the high school at seven o'clock A. M. A few questions were selected from each list, and at once mimeographed by some stenographers. We prided ourselves that no one could get an inkling of what the questions were to be because they were only put in shape that morning. We had nine hundred men and women taking the examination. Every room in the building was crowded. We had one person in charge of each room, who had a printed list of the rules of the examination, and I made a talk to each group of applicants.

To show how necessary it was to hold an examination to discover the grade of intelligence of some of the applicants for the position of probation officer, I quote a few of the answers to some of our questions:

Q. What is the theory of the Juvenile Court?

A. "The theory of the Juvenile Court is to sublet the job of reformation to a person."

Q. What is a dependent?

A. "A dependent is one who is reliable. A delinquent is a no-account."

Q. Why do you wish to become a probation officer?

A. "I seek the position of probation officer because I feel that I am particularly fitted for the work, having had charge of four boys who bid fair to be criminals, and made priests out of all four."

Q. Why do you wish to become a probation officer?

A. "I seek the position of probation officer because I like the uplift business."

After the examination was over the papers were locked in a vault. It took our committee six weeks to read these papers; each one was read aloud and was marked as the majority of the committee voted. An oral examination was then held and out of the nine hundred applicants only eighty-one passed the examination.

Some of the people who did not pass were very irate, one man going so far as to threaten to shoot me if I did not re-mark his paper; for two or three weeks he dogged my footsteps and many a time I have gone out of the back door of Hull-House as he entered the front door. On one occasion, when I finished a speech before a large audience, several of my friends literally grabbed me and hustled me out of the door into a machine; when I asked why I was being thus summarily ejected, I was told that this man was waiting for me in the room and was vowing vengeance.

One day this man came into my office and told me I need not be afraid, he was not going to kill me. I looked into his eyes and said I was not afraid. I trust this was one of the lies which angels are said to blot out by tears. The man also said,

"I would like to kill you but I would be found out if I did, so I want to tell you that I am not going to do it." I said I was thankful for this kindness and appreciated the consideration shown me. This individual saw no humor in the situation and left the room, slamming the door.

I have sometimes thought that if I had talked more with this man and been a little more sympathetic with him concerning his failure to pass the examination, we would not have had such a disagreeable time.

Talking out things is certainly a great safety valve. Miss Addams realized this at Hull-House and has sometimes been criticized for allowing associations, whose ideas were most radical, to meet there and express their opinions. Miss Addams felt, however, that if the people who belonged to these organizations were allowed to talk freely, they would not be apt to do anything more, and this certainly is the view held by the English authorities who allow those great open meetings in Hyde Park where anyone who wishes may express freely and without molestation his opinion concerning the government.

CHAPTER VII

THE JUVENILE PROTECTIVE ASSOCIATION*

When the Juvenile Protective Association was formed it seemed as if it would not be difficult to find out what was wrong in the city and to set it right, but such a number of conditions injurious to children were immediately uncovered by our officers that we hardly knew where to begin; and when our office was opened we received any number of complaints concerning children who were ill-used or who were exposed to temptation. Many of these complaints were anonymous, sent to us by neighbors who were afraid to have their names used, but almost all of them proved to be accurate in their statements. For example, a complaint would come in from a neighbor who from her back window had seen the child of a woman who lived next door tied in the back yard all day, until the mother came back from work. In one instance, a neighbor, looking through the window of the house next door to her, saw a child tied to the leg of a table, where she

*Many of my experiences with the Juvenile Protective Association have appeared not only in pamphlet form but in a book entitled "Safeguards for City Youth at Work and at Play," published by Macmillan Company in 1914.

remained all day. When we investigated that case we found that the child's back had been permanently injured through having been tied in this position.

The association started dividing the city into districts, each of these districts having a paid officer whose duty it was to keep children out of disreputable ice cream parlors, candy stores and pool rooms, and to try in every way to protect and safeguard the children and young people. For several reasons, it was found very expensive to keep up these district leagues, and after a while they were dropped, although they had many merits. The association then made a trial of what it called the Block System, which was a plan by which every member of the association was given a definite piece of work. This person was expected to know the conditions in his block. He was asked, first, to make a survey of it, noting all vacant lots, pool rooms, dance halls, theaters, houses, shops, playgrounds and churches. He was furnished a little pamphlet issued by the association, written by me, and was asked to report back any injurious conditions found in his block. He was also expected to suggest constructive measures as to whether vacant lots could be turned into playgrounds or churches induced to open their rooms for recreation purposes, etc. At one time we had fifteen hundred blocks under observation, but after the novelty of the work had worn off people began gradually giving up these blocks and this part of the work ceased. We now have specialized officers. One attends to the dance halls, another looks out for runaway girls, another visits disreputable cabarets and cafés and still another is interested in boys' gangs and so on.

Work among gangs is most necessary, when we consider that in 1925 the Board of Education of Chicago was said to have appropriated $100,000 to replace broken windows in the school buildings of the city, mostly broken by gangs of boys who stormed the buildings.

This reminds me of the time when the Juvenile Protective Association was trying to get the school buildings opened in the evening for purposes of recreation. We had secured the consent of the Board of Education to have one school in a congested part of the city, and we advertised that the building would be open that evening and that there would be moving pictures and interesting talks. The school house was crowded not only inside but out, by those who could not get in. Those outside hurled jeers of defiance at those inside, they punctuated their remarks with volleys of stones which broke every window in the school building. When the time came for the meeting to break up, we did not dare let the children leave the building until we had smuggled a small boy out the basement door to get the police. When they arrived they dispersed the outside crowd and those inside were allowed to go home. It is needless to say that the Board of Education did not give us another school building for our activities and this incident put a stop, for a time, to the opening of the schools in the evening for recreational purposes.

We found that the young people were attending dance halls at this time, in such numbers that the officers of the association made an investigation of something like five hundred of these halls. Indeed, we spent a great deal of time on these places. No other association had ever before made any report concerning them, to my knowledge. We found they were dens of iniquity. Liqour was sold in them, no drinking water was procurable, the dressing rooms were in a very unsanitary condition. The halls were dirty and filled with dissolute men and women who speedily corrupted decent young girls and boys who frequented them. Appeals to the dance hall owners brought about no results. Prosecutions on the ground of selling liquor seemed to get nowhere. At one time we had something like forty-nine samples of liquor purchased by our investigators in these dance halls and cabarets. When they went to court on their cases the judge asked how they knew that the liquor purchased *was* liquor. He said it must be analyzed. We had to pay a chemist to appear in court and to testify that the samples of whiskey *were* liquor. The cases were continued so many times that we finally had to give up the matter and, as I remember it, only won something like two cases out of the forty-nine. Then we began on another tack and have been most successful with the public dance halls, not because of our own efforts, but because we enlisted the sympathy and the coöperation of the dance hall keepers themselves, who, at the suggestion of Miss Jessie Binford, our superintendent, formed an association called the Dance Hall and Ball Room Managers' Association. This association keeps the dance halls, which it controls, decent. In each one of these halls there is a chaperone recommended by us. These chaperones are paid for by the Ball Room Association. They also give the Juvenile Protective Association donations for the salary of a dance hall officer. They pay for the upkeep of a motor which she uses. She visits all the dance halls, reports anything that is wrong to the managers, and they immediately make it right. If an employee is found who for any reason has taken any liberties with a patron of the dance hall, that man is immediately discharged and blacklisted so that he is not employed by any other hall.

We have always kept a record of the dance halls of the city, and many a mother calls us up to know if such and such a hall is a respectable place for her daughter to attend. It is always very hard to make parents understand that children must have a certain amount of recreation. One mother said to us, with tears in her eyes, that she could not do anything with her daughter. She had taken her to

Sunday School, had seen that she attended every church service on Sunday, also Wednesday and Friday evenings, she had taught her many hymns and saw that she said her prayers and yet the girl still wanted to dance.

I have often visited some of the better dance halls and I was always much impressed by the crowds of young people who attended them. In one dance hall where I had taken a party one evening, the proprietor came to me to say that if I would like to make a speech he would stop the dancing and let me do it. I was horrified by the idea and declined with thanks. This same dance hall has a large sign in it saying, "This dance hall is approved by the Juvenile Protective Association."

We found that so many boys and girls were engaged in street trading that, after many conferences with the mayor, the city attorneys and heads of some of the big dailies, an ordinance was finally put through the Council which prohibits boys under fourteen years of age from selling any papers on the streets before five o'clock in the morning, and after eight o'clock at night, and this ordinance also prohibits any girl under the age of eighteen years from selling any merchandise whatever on Chicago streets. This ordinance has been fairly well enforced, and has been an invaluable aid in protecting boys and girls.

We have received many complaints in regard to children who frequent the news alleys connected with some of the larger papers. After reports had been made, these places were cleaned up but it takes constant vigilance to see that they are kept so. Once, when we were talking to some newspaper managers in regard to their news alleys where the walls were covered with obscene pictures and writings, the floors covered with filth, and which were frequented by the toughest youths of the city, a manager told us he let his children wait in these alleys every night when they drove down for him before he was ready to go home. I told him that of course if he wanted his children to be in that kind of a place I presumed there was no law to stop him, but that I was sorry for the children.

We have made several investigations in regard to baby farms, and found that children were boarded in homes utterly unfit for habitation. Many of the children died from lack of medical care or from starvation or negligence. We were able to secure the removal of over one hundred children from these farms and owing to this effort the City Council passed an ordinance providing that baby farms, where more than three children were kept, must secure a license.

We had such large numbers of cases brought into court under the Contributing to Delinquency and Dependency Law that we asked for the establishment of a separate court where all such cases could be tried, as we found that cases were being taken into first one court and then another, and the punishment for offenders was most uneven. We were successful in getting a branch of the Municipal Court established, known as the Court of Domestic Relations, and we paid the salary of its first social secretary. I hesitate to say that the Court of Domestic Relations was established at the suggestion of this association, because it has been claimed by many politicians and several organizations. However, I do know that Mrs. James Britton, the Superintendent of the Juvenile Protective Association, and I begged Judge Olson, the Municipal Chief Justice, to establish it, and that I went on to New York to visit the Court of Domestic Relations there, and I reported what I learned at that court to Judge Olson, who then said that he would establish such a court here.

We have also enlisted the help of the Pool Room and Billiard Hall Managers' Association. These people are most anxious to have the pool rooms decent. They coöperate with us and do what they can to make the pool rooms respectable.

I have had some amusing times reporting stage children. I remember on one occasion I reported a little girl whom I had seen in a play and I found afterwards that she was a dwarf and over twenty-one years of age! At another time, Mrs. Fiske had been using a little child in one of her plays, and I went to the theatre that night to see if she had given up using the child. She had complied with our request but had an eighteen year old boy in his place. She had evidently chosen a large one to make the thing look ridiculous, and when he said his prayers by her knee and sat on her lap he almost swamped her, and I could not help having a hearty laugh at my own expense.

At one time we found so many young girls who were in disreputable houses that we felt sure that vice was greatly on the increase. Some of the other organizations in the city were making reports to the effect that there was very little commercialized vice, and in order to prove that our contention was correct we secured one of the best investigators from the American Social Hygiene Association of New York. He came here and visited about two hundred houses of prostitution. In order to be sure that his report was perfectly accurate, he was followed by two of our own men who confirmed everything that he had reported. When the report was ready I went with the superintendent of the association and presented it to Judge McKinley, then Chief Justice of the Criminal Court of Chicago. He read the report and advised us to present the facts to the grand jury. This was done, and brought about a great deal of publicity. I remember the superintendent and I going to the Criminal Court Building and being snapped by many photographers in the hallways as we made our way into the judge's office. Later on the report was presented to the grand jury, they were charged by Judge McKinley concerning the subject but rendered no true bills. Judge McKinley then summoned a second grand jury and the charges were again presented to them. Again they found no bills. Then Judge McKinley called us in again and told us that if we found that the Chief of Police or any police captains were not doing their duty, we were to summon them into court and he would act as the examining magistrate. This plan worked most effectively. At once the Chief of Police gave orders that all disreputable houses were to be closed. Police were stationed at the front and back doors to see that this order was obeyed. The Chief of Police claimed that crimes against life and property would undoubtedly increase since so many of his officers were watching these houses. Statistics, however, showed in the next few weeks that crime had decreased something like thirty-two per cent. Many of the people who ran these disreputable houses gave them up and although some of them may have reopened in different parts of the town, there has been a noticeable improvement and there is much less commercialized vice now than then.

The association kept one officer working in the jail. She found that many boys were railroaded into the penitentiary because there was no one except perhaps an indifferent lawyer to defend them. A pamphlet was, therefore, written, setting forth the conditions of these boys and the data here gathered helped in the establishment of the Boys'

Court, where boys between the ages of seventeen and twenty-one, commonly known as the juvenile adult, could be tried. I remember that I was presiding at a big meeting of Suffragists in Washington. I had asked Judge Olson to speak there. In the course of his speech, he said, "Mrs. Bowen has made me establish a Court of Domestic Relations, and now she wants a Boys' Court, and, by Jove, I'm going to do it!" I rose from my seat and said, "Judge Olson, that's a promise, and we're going to hold you to it." He remained true to his word, and shortly after the Boys' Court of Chicago was formed.

We furnished two full-time officers in this court for over a year, and one half-time officer. We provided the court with record cards and did everything in our power to see that the court was established on a firm basis. I spoke at the opening of the court, and was full of high hopes as to its future. These hopes have not always been realized because political appointments among the social workers in this and in other courts have not added to its efficiency.

We made an investigation of girls in fifty hotels and seventy-two restaurants, with a view to finding out how they were treated in these place of employment. We found that in many places the girls had wretched rooms, poorly ventilated, and they ate only the come-backs from the tables. Protests to some of the hotels and restaurants brought about some changes and the Junior League of Chicago, in response to a request from me representing this association, then established a rest room on South State Street for waitresses who are employed in restaurants and who, between the hours of two and five o'clock every day, have no place to go and no means of resting. This rest room was continued for several years, until one was opened by the waitresses' union and the one run by the Junior League was then discontinued. The Junior League have always since that time given us the salary of an officer who has devoted her time to removing beggars and child traders from the streets and to keeping little children off the stage.

One day a woman came into the office, naturally very much disturbed because she had sent her little girl to have her picture taken, and the photographer had shown her some very indecent pictures and begged her to have her photograph taken without any clothes. We then made an investigation of three hundred and sixty-eight photograph galleries. Seven proprietors of these galleries were sent to the penitentiary.

We found that the waiting rooms of the large department stores were frequented by young girls, that white slavers often used these waiting rooms, made acquaintances with the girls and finally induced them to lead a disreputable life. We secured the information because a daughter of one of our directors was at one time in one of these rooms.

She was approached by a good looking young man who scraped up an acquaintance with her and began to tell her how much money she could earn in another position. The association made an investigation of these different places, the stores coöperating with them, and in consequence sixteen men and women were arrested, tried, convicted and sent to the penitentiary. The department stores on State Street then gave one thousand dollars a year, but later we lost this subscription after I had addressed a large meeting composed of department store clerks, and urged organization upon them. I did this because these clerks were at that time very much under-paid. They had no redress, no opportunities for securing better wages, no grievance committee to which they could report floor managers who took liberties with them, or anything which happened while they were at their work. Cards were circulated among the stores saying that this large meeting was to be held and was to be addressed by me. In consequence, I lost my thousand dollars and always felt sure that it was because of my activities in this line.

At one time some public school teachers complained to us that their children had sore fingers, and that they could not find out the cause. A talk with some of the children showed that they were working in nut factories cracking nuts with hammers. We found that this nut cracking and picking was a tremendous industry and that there were something like forty such factories in Chicago. Children were employed in these places from four o'clock in the afternoon (when school was over) until midnight; the children often smashed their fingers as they worked through the early hours of the night in rooms laden with dust which came from cracked shells, and they doubtless inhaled much of this deleterious matter. Complaint to the factory inspector brought no result. The following July he made an investigation of these nut factories and reported no children were employed. As the nut cracking was done in the winter, it was no wonder that he did not find any children in the summer.

The Juvenile Protective Association then reported this matter to the federal authorities in Washington, they sent a government official here, who verified our investigation, and since it was at the time when the federal law provided that there should be a tax on all goods manufactured by children, shipped from state to state, all the factories involved were made to pay a tax, in consequence a more modern method of cracking nuts was used and the employment of children discontinued.

A well-known lawyer once asked Miss Addams and me and one or two other women if we would hear the story of a girl who had been found badly cut and locked in a bathroom of a hotel in this city. The girl, who was a modest looking little Irish girl, told us the story with downcast eyes and low and trembling voice. It was to the effect that a woman who kept a store in this hotel had lured her into the store and sold her to a white slaver who, after having assaulted her, locked her in a bathroom, slashed her with a razor and escaped through the transom of the bathroom. The details of this story were most revolting and the most terrible to which I ever listened, and when the girl had finished we felt that a horrible tragedy had been revealed. This girl was later examined at the Psychopathic Clinic, recently established through the kindness of Mrs. William H. Dummer, and it was found that her story was all a figment of her imagination. She had entered the hotel and gone into a public bathroom, removed her clothes, wounded herself severely with a razor in order that she might be found there and make a sensation, which she certainly accomplished. The girl was deported and sent back to Ireland.

It is very difficult to judge, when stories of this kind are told you, whether they are accurate or not, and it was a great comfort when the Psychopathic Clinic was established, and such cases were sent there for trained men to diagnose.

For twenty-five years I have been president of this association, and during this time I have interviewed any number of girls and boys who have gone wrong, or who were on the road to delinquency. I have always felt that our public schools should be open in the evenings more than they are now, and that the churches should give more help in an effort to provide boys and girls with decent and enjoyable recreation.

Some time ago some one asked me how many souls I thought had been saved by the Juvenile Protective Association. My reply was that I did not know that we had ever saved any souls, but if we had kept one young boy or girl decent, we could feel that we had accomplished something.

Sometimes the children brought to us were so pathetic in their innocence that it seemed as if I could hardly stand it. One little girl of twelve with beautiful long curls down her back, had been put by her mother in a house of prostitution in Michigan. She had lived for two years with an old man and then the mother, wishing to get more money, sent her down to Chicago. She was met at the station by a "cadet." The little girl was so striking looking, with her long curls and innocent face, that she attracted the attention of a policeman. It seems that she, with another little girl who lived in the same house with her, had played dolls together and read the newspapers. This little girl had seen the picture of Miss Jane Addams in the paper quite frequently, so she always played she was Miss Addams. When she got to Chicago and the policeman asked her where she was going, she said to Miss Addams, and he took her by the hand and led her to Hull-House, who turned her over to us. We boarded her with one of our officers, and after a time she was sent to a convent. The little girl was so young that her terrible experiences had apparently made no impression upon her.

I was at one time a member of the advisory committee who looked at the very bad moving pictures concerning which the police censors were doubtful. This was done at the City Hall, and I found it most disagreeable. I have always hated moving pictures since then, because all those that I saw were quite horrid.

The association made an investigation of two hundred girls working in factories. It found out some of the inconveniences and the injustices under which these girls labored, and it did what it could to adjust these difficulties. A very handsome little girl was in the office one morning talking with an officer of the association who had found her flirting with a stranger outside a factory where she worked. The officer said to her, "You must not flirt with strange men," and the little girl replied, "Why, I did not mean to flirt, but I just cannot make my eyes behave," then looking at the rather pretty officer who had her in charge, she said roguishly, "I guess you have some trouble that way sometimes."

For many years I have held luncheons at Hull-House for the officers of the Juvenile Protective Association. In this way I become personally acquainted with them. They talked quite freely about their work and listening to them and reading their monthly reports of what is going on in different parts of the city gives me a general insight into conditions. We always invite to these luncheons outside people, some of the dance hall proprietors, the billiard and pool room officers and managers, and perhaps some police women or the States Attorney, or officials from the Juvenile Court, and many other organizations with whom the Juvenile Protective Association frequently comes into contact. These luncheons are very illuminating, and at the same time extremely interesting.

When Mayor Harrison was persuaded, by the united efforts of many organizations in the city, to put on women police, I invited them to take luncheon with me once a month at Hull-House. I tried to put before them some ideals as to their work, to discuss with them some of the problems of the day. After a while, however, they were withdrawn, I suppose by the chief of their department, and since then I have only been able to get hold of one or two at a time. It was a great disappointment to find that soon after they had been appointed, they had been put at revolver practice, and were being sent to investigate disreputable cafés and to walk beats in lonely parts of the town at night. I remember going to see Mayor Harrison about this matter and he was as indignant as I was, and promptly gave the order which removed them from such dangerous practice. Women police are not intended to act as vice investigators, to arrest criminals or to regulate traffic, but they are supposed to be in the dance halls, the restaurants, the cabarets, the theatres, any place where young people congregate, and to be constantly on the lookout for the dangers which so often beset them.

The standard of examinations for police women is not sufficiently high in Chicago to attract women of education and refinement. The Juvenile Protective Association has frequently tried to have this standard raised, but so far has been unsuccessful.

In connection with the Juvenile Protective Association I wrote many pamphlets, which were published by the association and widely circulated. These pamphlets were written after I had read reports of perhaps a special investigation made by one of our officers, and they dealt with innumerable subjects, "The Welfare of Children," "The Block System," "Legislative Needs in Illinois," "Study of Bastardy Cases," "The Straight Girl on the Crooked Path," "The Department Store Girl," "Girls in Hotels and Restaurants, Dance Halls," etc.; I remember one pamphlet directed against a corrupt administration, which I called "The Road to Destruction Made Easy in Chicago." The printer sent it back to me with the inquiry, "Did I wish the cover to read as it appeared?" "The Road to Destruction Made Easy in Chicago by Louise de

Koven Bowen." Needless to say I immediately made a change in the cover.

In my work along various lines, I have often had to report and prosecute people who were connected with the vice interests of the city, and I have sometimes wondered why I did not have more threats. On several occasions, I did receive threatening letters, and once I received a warning not to open any mail which looked suspicious. Shortly after, a bulky package was received at the Juvenile Protective Association, addressed to one of our investigators. It was taken to the police department and after putting it in water, was opened, and was found to contain a bomb which would have exploded had it been opened by the investigator to whom it was addressed.

At another time when the Juvenile Protective Association had been making vice investigations in the city, I was awakened at three o'clock in the morning by a knock on my door. I opened it and found my maid looking pale and frightened. In a shaking voice she said, "There is a bomb in the vestibule and the night watchman wants to know what to do with it." It seemed to me an absurd question to ask, but I hastily said, "Tell him to take it away." The maid dashed down the stairs, and I rushed to the back of the house, thinking if I was going to be blown up I would get as far as possible from the bomb, but my curiosity overcame me. I went to the front window to see what was happening, and saw the watchman marching down the street carrying a basket in one end of which was a large paving stone, and in the other something wrapped in a black cloth about as big as a man's head. The night watchman soon returned, and I called from the window, "Was that a bomb?" He said, "No, it was only a kitten someone intended to drown." Evidently the murderer had not the heart to carry out his plan, and the kitten was deposited at my door. I did not, however, have a very high idea of the intelligence of a night watchman who would ring the doorbell in order to know what to do with a bomb found in a vestibule.

I once received a letter threatening to have my grandchildren kidnapped. It was signed with the black hand, and we were very unhappy in consequence for some time. The children were never allowed out alone, they were always followed by a man wherever they went. We put detectives on the job and a very skillful member of the force found that the letter had come from a man who was confined in an insane asylum.

In all parts of the city, we have found the forces for good less well organized and active than those that work injury and destruction. The bright lights and open doors of cheap theatres, dance halls and cabarets urge a constant invitation upon the boys and girls whose dreary homes and love of excitement drive them into the streets for recreation, while against these lurid and dangerous pleasures, wholesome and well-regulated amusements are negligible quantities.

In looking over my twenty-five years as president of this association, I find great changes. The dangers for the youth of the city which were so apparent twenty-five years ago are not now so frequently encountered. The temptations are perhaps more subtle. There is no segregated district now. The houses of prostitution are fewer. There are very few bad dance halls. I do not suppose that any of the photograph galleries or places of that kind are disreputable, and yet there are many dangers. The motor car has brought many new perils in its wake. The little towns outside, near Chicago, are full of roadhouses, and the young people can get there in a very short time. They are more secure from observation there. The country roads are not well policed. Even the cars themselves are sometimes disreputable resorts. Not very long ago, coming back from one of the North Shore towns, I counted seventeen of these cars parked on a side road late at night.

If the women police of Chicago could have as their dean someone who is well trained for preventive work among children and young people, and if these women police could be sent all over the city just as the officers of the Juvenile Protective Association are now, then we would have a better chance of guarding children, and the expense of this protection would be borne by the municipality and not by a private organization.

Children hold the future of the nation in their hands. If they are allowed to deteriorate physically and morally, our national life will inevitably suffer.

CHAPTER VIII

PRESIDENTS, MEETINGS AND SPEECHES

With a record of fifty years of social service behind me, I feel as if I should have met most of the prominent men of the country, but I have always been a home lover, and, though my friends laugh at me when I say it, I have always been rather shy, and have not wanted to meet strangers. I have followed closely the history of our country and been greatly interested in what was going on at Washington. Abraham Lincoln was President when I was a little girl, and I used to see a good deal of him because his little boy, Tad Lincoln, was about my age, and a great friend of mine. The Lincolns, when they came to Chicago, always stopped at a little hotel known as the Clifton House, on the corner of Madison Street and Wabash Avenue. It was only two doors away from my grandfather's house where I lived, and Tad and I often played together in the Lincolns' apartments, where Mr. Lincoln would sometimes go in and out, giving me a kind word as he passed.

One day my mother came into my room and throwing herself on her knees beside the bed said, "Our beloved President is assassinated!" I was perhaps too young to realize what it meant, but I wept with her because she was so overcome with grief. A few days later the body of Lincoln lay in state in the court house of the city, and I was taken by my father to see him. The streets were full of people, almost all of whom were dressed in black; the flags were at half-mast; the women all looked as though they had been crying. Anyone would have known at once that a great calamity had overtaken the city and the nation. At the door of the court house we stood amid an orderly crowd and slowly pushed our way into the hall and then into a room dimly lighted and guarded by soldiers. At the end of the room lay the casket with the body of our great President. My father lifted me upon his shoulders, and as we passed by in solemn silence, I looked down from my height upon the majestic face of our martyred President.

My next presidential recollection is that of President Arthur, who spent some time at Bar Harbor, where we had a summer place. I remember a reception was given him there, and all the young men were much troubled because they had no dress suits at this island resort, and felt they ought not to be introduced to a President unless they were properly clad.

President Roosevelt I had met many times. My first acquaintance with him was when I was invited with about two hundred other people from all parts of the United States, to go to a Conference on

Dependent Children held at the White House. This was at a time when the advantages of home care for children were being put forward as so much better than those of orphanages, although when I went to the White House and knew that Mr. Roosevelt was to open the meeting, I felt that in all probability he would not know very much about the subject. We were all gathered in one of the big parlors awaiting his advent. The door was suddenly opened. First came an aide-de-camp in a brilliant uniform, and then the President. With a word of greeting, he took from his pocket a speech on the treatment of dependent children and read it with much fervor and enthusiasm. This speech had the newest and most modern ideas on the treatment of dependents, and was literally an eye-opener to most of the social workers present. After finishing his speech, the President asked for comments or questions. They were fired at him from all parts of the room, and he responded with great courtesy and wisdom.

I had the pleasure of campaigning in Chicago for Mr. Roosevelt, and it was the first time I had ever done any campaign speaking. Most of the meetings were held in vacant stores during the day, where one had to speak very loud in order to drown the noise of the traffic from outside. It was a great pleasure to speak for a man whose career had been so remarkable, and whose ideals I so much admired. It was a real blow that he was not elected. Later on, I had the pleasure of giving him a dinner at my house. About forty people sat down, and Mr. Roosevelt made a most excellent speech in which he said that if he had been elected he would have put a woman in his cabinet.

Some time later Mr. Roosevelt called one afternoon at my house. I had about a dozen women in my dining room at that time, writing invitations for something, and I asked him if he would come out and be introduced, and he said he would with pleasure. He came into the room, shook hands with everyone, and was most delightful in everything he had to say. I was one of his great admirers, and considered that his loss was an irreparable one to the United States.

I saw President Wilson two or three times when I was invited to the White House with different associations which were meeting at that time in Washington. On one of these occasions we were all shown into one of the large rooms in the White House, and suddenly a door was thrown open. Mrs. Wilson came in first, followed by Mr. Wilson. He made a short speech to us and shook hands most cordially with everyone.

When President Harding called the Disarmament Conference he was kind enough to appoint me one of the four women bidden to that conference. Because of some family reasons I could not leave home at that time, and so was obliged to decline, and someone else was appointed in my place. It was one of the greatest disappointments of my life not to sit in at that notable gathering. Not that I could have been of any use, but it was a historic occasion, and one long to be remembered by every loyal American.

Later on, President Harding appointed me as the only governmental delegate from the United States to represent this country at the Pan-American Conference of Women which was held in Baltimore in 1923. I remember with a great deal of amusement my arrival in Baltimore. I went to the hotel where the conference was to be held, only to be told that the crowds attending it were so great that the place of meeting had been changed to the Century Theatre. When I asked where this theatre was, the kind woman who manned the hostess's desk, said to me, "I am going there myself, and I will take you with me." As we came out of the hotel I started to call a cab, but being a thrifty person she remonstrated, and said, "You must save your money for the League of Women Voters, under whose auspices the Pan-American Conference is held." We then stopped a street car and she hustled me in, where I hung onto a strap for some time. Then, a kind man giving me a seat, I vanished from the woman's sight. When we reached the Century Theatre, imagine my horror to have this kind woman look down the car and say in loud tones, "Where's the old woman I put on this car?" I meekly got up and said, "Here I am." She thought she had lost me,

THE COURT AT HULL-HOUSE.

and then, feeling a little embarrassed, she said, "Oh, I didn't mean you. I put two old ones on." This I knew to be untrue. She then asked me whom I represented at the conference, and I answered promptly, "The United States." "Oh, dearie," said she, "we all come from the United States!" After that she left me, and when I finally took my place on the stage under the banner of the United States, I wondered what she thought.

This conference was extremely interesting, representing something like twenty-two South American countries. As I went on the stage I was told by the chairman that after all the twenty-two delegates had spoken I was to gather everything together and give a synopsis of what had been said. Imagine my dismay when I found that most of the delegates spoke either in their own language or else in such broken English that it was impossible for me to understand! In the end, I gave a welcome to the foreign delegates. Later I spoke on "Child Welfare in the United States," "Women in Industry in the United States," "Traffic in Women in the United States," and "The Political Status of Women in the United States."

Some of the things the delegates said were most amusing, although they did not mean them to be so. For example, on the subject, "Women in Industry," the foreign women always called it "Women in Labor." At that time Brazil was having trouble with a neighbor, and the delegates from the two countries did not like sitting next to each other. I found myself in the capacity of a peace-maker many times, and I had to rearrange seats so that only those who were sympathetically inclined toward one another sat together.

The whole congress was most interesting in the point of view expressed by various foreign delegates, all of whom represented a high order of intelligence, and one could not but admire the versatility with which they spoke of what was being done in their own countries on the various questions brought before the congress. Such conferences tend to make a friendly feeling and the fact that women get together in this way and learn from each other, will certainly make for solidarity among the nations of the earth.

When I was president of the Women's Roosevelt Republican Club, it gave a luncheon to Mrs. Calvin Coolidge, wife of the President of the United States. I had the pleasure of talking with Mrs. Coolidge during the hour preceding the luncheon when I was presenting members of the board to her, in the Presidential suite of the Congress Hotel. The hall outside was crowded with sightseers, and when the time came to go to the big room where thirteen hundred women were awaiting Mrs. Coolidge, Mrs. McCormick took her by one arm and her special attendant, who goes everywhere with her, a tall fine-looking man, took hold of her other arm. They hurried her so fast through the crowd that I was literally obliged to run to keep up with them. I sat next to Mrs. Coolidge during the luncheon, and introduced her. I, therefore, had a good opportunity to continue the acquaintance. I found her most charming, very dignified, but with a keen sense of humor.

While we were at luncheon Mrs. Coolidge had a policewoman directly behind her, and several policemen in the balcony just over her head. A well-known woman in the audience came up to the table where we sat and began to talk to Mrs. Coolidge, much to the annoyance of us all. As this woman went back into the audience, both the committeewomen from Illinois (who sat on the other side of Mrs. Coolidge) and I looked rather annoyed and Mrs. Coolidge, sensing our feelings, gave a little shudder and said, "It seems rather chilly around here."

In my capacity as president of various organizations, I was occasionally asked to preach sermons and this I greatly enjoyed, because it gave me an opportunity of demonstrating to clergymen that I believed in short sermons. I remember my chagrin on one occasion when I was to speak in an Episcopal Church in Chicago, when, after the service, the clergyman announced that as the sermon was to be preached by a woman it could not be given in the church, and he asked the congregation to adjourn to the Sunday School room by the side door. Needless to say, the congregation escaped on the way, and

I had only a small handful to whom to deliver my carefully prepared address. I reproached the clergyman afterwards, but was told that of course a woman could not speak in an Episcopal Church. However, all Episcopalians did not feel that way and I have often preached in Episcopal Churches in Chicago, not in the pulpit but standing just below the chancel.

I preached one Sunday morning before the Ethical Society and was afterwards told that it was customary to give the preacher twenty-five dollars for services rendered, but the gratification I felt was immediately removed by my being informed that it was also customary for the preacher to donate this twenty-five dollars to the settlement run by the society. I rose to the occasion and said I would be glad to give my fee to the settlement. The joke, however, came the following year when I received a letter from the Ethical Society reminding me that I had contributed twenty-five dollars to their settlement, and asking me to renew my subscription.

I have had all kinds of introductions for my speeches; one erudite club president, with many long words, introduced me as "The Woman Who Will Talk on the Prevention of Children." Of course she meant "Protection," but got a little mixed in her words. I remember another occasion where the Chairman had bothered me almost to death beforehand, asking for details of my life, and I felt sure she was going to give me a most glowing introduction. Her courage evidently failed at the last moment, as she stood up and pointing a shaking finger at me said: "This is Mrs. Bowen, I have forgotten what she is going to talk about."

I must not forget one introduction which made me feel most uncomfortable. I had gone to speak at the Detention Home which had recently moved into its new building, which I had been active in securing. The superintendent took me into a room where there were about sixty boys; they were all sitting around looking very sullen and most unhappy. The superintendent introduced me as "the kind lady who has made it possible for you to come to this nice place." Such fierce scowls were immediately bent upon me that it was all I could do to talk.

I was much chagrined one day to be invited by one of the large hotels on the outskirts of the city to come at noontime and preach a funeral sermon over a canary bird that had just died. The lady who gave me this invitation said the canary bird was a pet of the children in the hotel, and she felt she ought to get one of the best known women of the city to preach at its funeral. Needless to say I declined this invitation with some asperity, not feeling sure whether I had been insulted or complimented.

There are times when a speaker has her nerves sorely tried. One of those occasions was when a mouse played around in front of me when I was making an impassioned appeal for a most worthy cause; I had great difficulty in keeping my thoughts clear on this occasion. At another time, I was speaking at a meeting held on the top floor of a settlement house, and smoke began to pour up through the floor. I found it hard to continue while the cause of the fire was sought. Fortunately it proved to be only a smoky fireplace on the floor below.

Perhaps the hardest time I ever had to hold on to myself was while I was speaking in one of the community centers on the West Side. It was in the evening; the room contained perhaps a thousand people. There was a tremendous thunder storm and suddenly the lights went out not only in the building but in the street, and we were in absolute darkness except for the flashes of lightning. I made a joke of the fact that I would not now know whether the audience went to sleep or not, then I applied myself most diligently to being as interesting as possible. Just as I finished my speech, after perhaps half an hour had elapsed, the lights came on, and there had been no panic.

I have done some introducing myself, and profiting by my own experience have always tried to be as brief as possible. On one occasion, at the Auditorium Theatre, when I was introducing Theodore Roosevelt, the audience would not let me speak and kept calling, "We want Teddy! We want Teddy!" I stopped and said, "You cannot have him until I have properly introduced him," whereupon they let me finish my introduction.

On another occasion I introduced Mr. Taft who had just finished his term as President of the United States; he was speaking before the Chicago Equal Suffrage Association, and I started by saying, "Mr. Taft, I am going to introduce the Chicago Equal Suffrage Association to *you,*" whereupon the whole audience arose and bowed and then sat down.

I have presided at a great many meetings and have always been most anxious to follow very closely the program. On one occasion I was presiding in a theatre and various aldermen were to speak. They had been told they could only speak five minutes and a bell rang when they had talked four minutes. They were rather disposed to take advantage when they saw a woman presiding. One alderman did not heed the bell, but continued to speak. I said, "Please sit down. Your time is up." He paid no attention. Without considering the matter seriously, but in my effort to make him sit down, I leaned over and took him by the coat tail and, giving it a vigorous pull, said, "Sit down!" It was all that was needed, for what man could continue a speech with the chairman pulling his coat tails? After this every alderman adhered strictly to the rule.

Another time I had twelve speakers; each one was given three minutes. I took to the meeting a three-minute glass used for boiling eggs. I put it on the table and announced to each speaker that he could talk as long as the sand was running out; not a man took his eye off that sand glass, and the scheme worked most beautifully.

One of the most nervous times presiding that I ever experienced was when I was asked to preside at a meeting of Republicans held in the Auditorium Theatre. Senator Medill McCormick was the speaker, and I was asked to introduce him. The hall was crowded—not a vacant seat. The day before I had publicly endorsed the election of a Democratic alderman who had served the city faithfully. The Republicans were so angry with me for what they called "party disloyalty," that I was told, as I went on the stage that night, that there were two hundred men in the audience who were going to break up the meeting. I found I had a good-sized gavel on the desk, and, although I felt a little anxious, nothing happened. On another occasion I was caught without a gavel, and this led to my undoing. It was at a meeting on the High Cost of Living. Professor Irving Fisher of Yale, Miss Jane Addams and several other notables were to speak. A man in the audience arose and started a personal attack on me. I had no gavel with which to silence him, and he could talk louder than I. As a result the whole house was in an uproar, the man rushed for the stage, two soldiers in the front row jumped upon it, and, much to my disgust, hustled me off to the wings. The man addressed the audience from the stage until we finally lowered the curtain and cut him off from the audience. I have always felt that the break-up of this meeting was because I had no gavel, but possibly it had to do with the fact that the men had returned from the war disheartened and disillusioned. There was no work for them and they very likely resented well-to-do people talking to them on the subject of economy.

On one occasion I was talking before a meeting composed entirely of clergymen. I was describing some very terrible conditions in a certain part of the city, and they all seemed much horrified but rather removed from the subject. When I left the room one of the clergymen opened the door for me and said, "I have been very much interested in your speech and I thank God every night that my parish has no places such as you describe." I asked him where his parish was. He told me, and I replied, "My dear sir, you would better pray God to help you clean up your district, for that is the identical one I have been discussing." I left him looking very much as if a pail of cold water had been poured over him.

Meetings are difficult to manage. People come late and go early. The chairman has to fight indifference and criticism. She has to have always with her a fund of patience, and, above all, she must not lose her sense of humor.

Speakers are often imposed upon; they are asked to come early and to sit through a mass of reports in which they are not interested, and they sometimes spend several hours in order to give a ten minute talk and put their message before a small audience. An illustration of this occurred in the early days of the Juvenile Court when Judge Mack, Mrs. Harry Hart and I were invited to talk before a club on the far West Side. When we arrived, each of us was astonished to find the others. The audience must also have felt that there were too many speakers, as only five women were present to hear about the Juvenile Court. All of which makes me feel that there should be an organization for the protection of speakers.

CHAPTER IX

SUFFRAGISTS AND STOCKHOLDERS

The question of Equal Suffrage had never interested me until I read in the papers about the English women who were fighting so hard to get it that they chained themselves to an iron fence in one of the big parks in London; thus secured by chains they addressed large numbers of people, and when the police arrested them, they found they were padlocked to the fence and the keys could not be found; as I remember, the police had to use files before they could pry away the indefatigable orators. I was so much impressed by these women that I thought there must be a good deal in a cause which would make them go through an ordeal of this kind. Shortly after, I was asked to talk to a big audience in Bowen Hall, and I took as my subject "Courage," and in speaking I announced that I was so thrilled by the courage of the English Suffragists that I had become a Suffragist myself, and intended to work for Suffrage in this country. I happened to see my husband's face in the crowd and I could see it drop as I made the announcement. Later he said to me, "Another new thing?" New things came fast at this time; old ideas were changing, new methods were coming in; women were beginning to be independent in thought and action, and they claimed equal rights with the men.

Miss Addams had been for a long time a Suffragist, and told me how glad she was I had become one. I remember how pleased I was that day because she told me she liked my speech so much and that even she had felt the need for it. I then joined the Illinois Suffrage Association, and was almost immediately made vice president of it; later I became president of the Chicago Equal Suffrage Association and held this position many years. This association gave courses of lectures on matters of current interest, and was constantly getting in new members and raising money for the Suffrage cause. About this time I went to Philadelphia with Miss Addams to the first National Woman's Suffrage Convention I had ever attended. Dr. Anna Howard Shaw was the valiant old war horse who then presided over the Suffrage destinies in our country. I admired immensely her knowledge of parliamentary law, her wonderful command of words, her ability to speak on almost every subject, the kindly criticism and fun which she everlastingly poked at the men, and the dominating power which she showed in every convention over which she presided. At this convention I was elected one of the auditors of the National Woman's Suffrage Association. I served for two years on this board, attending the meetings every month, which were usually held in New York. There were times when all the board would make a tour of the country and when we would speak in places such as Carnegie Hall, New York, the Opera House in Philadelphia, and in large churches and halls in almost all the big cities of the South and East. My subject was always "The Woman in the Home," and I can remember some meetings where we not only spoke in the opera house but went to overflow meetings afterwards, and even addressed crowds from soap boxes on the street corners. It was a very exciting time, but never can I remember having been treated with disrespect by the crowds of people who came to hear us. Our audiences consisted mostly of women, but men were often present; if a man attempted to hiss or make any objection to what was said, he was promptly put down by the hundreds of women who turned upon him.

I was on the national board when Miss Alice Paul left the national association and when she formed the Woman's Party I always felt that her interest and her ability should have been retained and that she should not have been allowed to form a separate party. During the latter part of my service on the national board several of the board came to me to ask if I would take the presidency. This I declined as I felt Dr. Shaw was the logical person to lead the Suffrage forces. It is always a regret to feel that this doughty pioneer died before she ever voted—before the cause to which she had given the best years of her life had been carried to victory.

Certainly the Suffragists were not only indefatigable workers but they never lost an opportunity to further their cause. When the conventions of the two great political parties were meeting, we always tried to get an audience and to get a Suffrage plank in the Republican or Democratic platform. At one time, when a Republican convention was held in Chicago, we had planned to descend upon the delegates with such a demand. We were told one night that the resolutions committee of the convention was meeting at the Congress Hotel. A number of us, perhaps fifty in all, went there and found ourselves outside the closed door of the room where the committee was meeting. We were in a tremendous crowd, packed closely against each other. It was very late—about 2 A. M. Miss Addams was just in front of me, and while we were standing there word came that she would introduce me when we entered the room and that I must make the speech. I felt considerably agitated at this shortness of opportunity for preparation. Just before the door was opened Miss Addams turned to me and said, "Something in the front of your dress has caught onto my back!" Sure enough, the lace in the front of my dress had caught on a button on the back of her dress. The door was being opened and we were literally pushed into the room. Miss Addams said, "Pull away! Pull away! We can't be hitched together this way." I said I couldn't, but just as the crowd surged forward and the door flew open I pulled myself away, only to find that I had left a large part of the front of my dress hanging to her back. She, of course, was oblivious of this addition to her costume, but I was painfully conscious of the hiatus in the front of mine, and when I addressed the Republican committee I had both hands clasped over my breast. They must have thought I was one of those temperamental persons who have to hold their hearts while they speak. Needless to say, they turned us down coldly, and I always felt that this *contretemps* did not help our cause.

During another convention we were to have a tremendous procession of women who were to walk down to the Coliseum where the Republican convention was being held. No one has seen it rain as hard as it did that day. The water came down in sheets; Michigan Avenue was wind swept and water swept. Through the puddles and the storm, blown and buffeted, wet and tired, five thousand women walked until they reached the Coliseum. Here occurred a very dramatic scene: An opponent of Suffrage had just announced that women did not want the franchise—that if they did they would take more pains to get it. At that moment there was a burst of music from the outside, the doors were thrown open and five thousand women trailed wetly and wearily into the Coliseum, with the demand that the Republicans put in their platform a plank for Equal Suffrage. Had the women planned it all beforehand it could not have been better staged; the fact that they had marched several miles on such a stormy day was proof positive that they certainly desired Equal Suffrage.

On another occasion I went with a delegation to Springfield, Illinois, to ask the State Senate to express themselves in favor of Equal Suffrage. We went first to the Capitol where we heard women derided from the platform and accused of being so violent in their efforts to get Suffrage that they were breaking laws and harming human beings. We were then referred to one of the committee rooms where a committee was sitting. As we waited, sounds of angry voices and much altercation came from the room; suddenly the door was opened and a man was literally kicked from the room, and was hurled with such violence against the wall that I remember blood splashes showed on the paint. We were then ushered into the room. I was spokesman, and in my remarks I took occasion to say that we had heard women were violent in their actions, but certainly we had never attempted any such violence as to eject a woman from a room so that even the walls were bloodstained. The men, however, looked on us with disdain, and as I returned to Chicago, I remember meeting Mr. Robert McCormick, editor of the *Tribune,* on the platform, who said, "What is the good of you women coming down here? You will never get what you want."

I attended almost all the Suffrage conventions with Miss Addams, and, because I was with her, met all the prominent people in the cities or the towns in which we visited. There were always dozens of people coming to our rooms to see her and to get her advice, and her interest in some cause, or to invite her to speak at some celebration. Our sitting room always looked like a doctor's waiting room as so many people came to see her, and there were times when I used crossly to insist that she could not be approached before eight o'clock in the morning or after midnight. About this time I went abroad with Miss Addams to attend, as a delegate from the Woman's National Suffrage Association, a convention to be held in Budapest, Hungary, of the International Suffrage Association. While we were in Paris I was taken ill and was unable to continue my journey.

It is perhaps a disappointment to find, now that women have the Suffrage, that they have not availed themselves as much as they should of the privileges of citizenship. They have not yet registered in sufficient numbers, and do not seem to realize their responsibilities. We know, however, that men were very slow in availing themselves of opportunities to vote. An able historian has recently noted that there has been a steady increase in the number of eligible voters in the United States and a steady decline in the percentage of those sufficiently interested in public affairs to go to the polls. In 1864 eighty-seven per cent. of our voting people cast their ballots at the polls, while in 1920, although twenty-six million people voted, including the newly enfranchised women, this was but fifty-three per cent of the total voting population of the country, a decline of thirty-four per cent. in fifty-six years! This decline of interest in our government constitutes a national menace; it is a challenge to the men and women of this country to participate more actively in this great business of guiding a democracy.

Women at this time were not allowed to serve as jurors, but a special ruling was made that they could serve as jurors in the Insane Court, and I was summoned on what was the first woman jury to sit in that court. It was a heartrending three days. The patients were brought before the court and were allowed to speak in their own defense. Sometimes it was very difficult to tell whether they were mentally unbalanced or not, and it was not a question that could be decided by a layman. It was rather a mortifying experience for the women jurors because the judge forgot we were there and made decisions himself. Two or three times we had to remind him of our presence and of the fact that we differed from him.

After we sat in the court, we were taken through the hospital where patients suffering from mental diseases were kept. Those who were confined to their beds had the jury visit them, and we would stand around these pathetic cases and talk to them, we would then give our opinion as to whether they were mentally unbalanced.

For this jury service women were paid two dollars a day, and it being the first money I had ever earned, I was determined to collect the six dollars due me. In order to do it I had to go to the County Building, wait in line for a long time, on one floor, until I received a little slip stating I had done jury service, then there was a long wait on another floor, where this slip was re-checked, then a visit to another window where I received a cashier's check, which I had to cash at a fourth window. It took me exactly one-half day to collect this six dollars, and I could not but wonder how a working man could afford to give so much time to collecting his money. While we were waiting for the vote we were by no means idle in public endeavor, as my experience as a stockholder illustrates. I owned stock in many of the big industrial corporations. Through my work at Hull-House I often was informed of conditions existing in some of these corporations deleterious to their employees. I could not help but feel that, as a stockholder and deriving my income from the profits of these corporations, I was at least partially responsible for the grievances of which I was constantly aware, and it seemed to me that as a stockholder I ought to bring about better conditions among working people. While I was wondering what I could do and how I could have any influence, one of my friends, Dr. Alice Hamilton of Hull-House, who was making investigations of industrial diseases for the federal government, asked me if I knew how bad were the conditions in the Pullman Company, in which I was a stockholder. She told me of men who frequently developed tuberculosis because of the work they were obliged to do in painting the washrooms of the Pullman cars, where the work was done indoors and where the men often contracted lead poisoning. She also gave me graphic descriptions of how the men (sometimes five in one day) got pieces of steel in their eyes, and how they were all treated by one physician, rather an old man who was not an eye specialist, and how, in consequence of his treatment, some of the men lost their sight. There were many other matters which came to her in the course of a study she had recently made in the works. I told her if she would get some one to go with her and make a thorough investigation of what was wrong with the Pullman Company I would take it up with the board of directors. She secured the services of one of the best research men in the city, and together they made a tour of the Pullman Company, and brought me a most detailed report. I sent this report to the president of the company. No reply. I then wrote again and said that if no attention was paid to the report I would see that it was given publicity in the papers. I saw several people who were stockholders in the Pullman Company, and they told me I might use their protests with mine. When I wrote the second time I said that I did not believe it would look well for a stockholder to object to taking his share of the profits because conditions were bad. I then received a prompt reply, and was asked, with Dr. Hamilton, to meet some of the officials of the company. We did meet with them; they were most courteous, and assured us they had made an investigation themselves and found things even worse than we had reported. They told us a change would be made at once, and almost immediately seventy-five thousand dollars was expended by the company. A hospital was built; five physicians, some of them specialists, were installed; Dr. Hamilton was asked for her recommendations concerning the men who worked with lead and she made several suggestions which almost obviated the danger of lead poisoning and tuberculosis. Altogether it was most gratifying.

Flushed with my victory over my first attempt at making suggestions of this kind, I then found the International Harvester Company in which I owned stock was running twine mills in which women worked all night. I collected all my arguments regarding women working at night; cited the various countries in the world where such employment of women was not allowed, and sent a letter to my personal friend, Mr. Cyrus H. McCormick, president of the International Harvester Company. I must say it took a great deal of courage to write this letter because the McCormicks were personal friends and I did not want to do anything that would injure or break that friendship. To my great relief, Mrs. McCormick called me up immediately over the telephone and said she was so grateful to me for having written the letter—that Mr. McCormick felt they should not employ women at night but that all the other directors did not feel the same way, and now that a stockholder had objected he would take up my letter with the board of directors. A short time after, Mr. McCormick asked if Miss Addams and I would attend a meeting of the heads of the departments of the company. We did so and met the executives connected with this great business enterprise. Mr. McCormick told us he had received my protest and assured us that within six weeks' time the twine mills would no longer employ women at night. We were much gratified at this action of the company and thanked him for it. He then asked me if I had anything more to suggest and I replied that I could wish that the International Harvester Company had a minimum wage for women. Mr. McCormick asked one of his men what was the lowest wage paid, and said they would take it under consideration. A few days later he stopped at my house to tell me that in the future the minimum wage for young women in his company would be eight dollars a week, which was then a sum on which a girl could live.

Later on I was asked by Mr. Charles M. Cabot, a broker of Boston, Massachusetts, who was a small stockholder of the United States Steel Corporation, if I would join with him in an effort to induce the steel company to give up the twelve-hour day.

Mr. Cabot had previously been very much interested in the atrocious housing conditions of the United States Steel Corporation in Pittsburgh, and had been able (through his efforts and those of other people) to have some of the buildings torn down there and some improvements made in the remainder. Meantime, Mr. Cabot's interest had become very much aroused, and "The Survey" called his attention to other conditions in the steel industry and he began an attack on the seven-day week. He won a victory within two years.

Mr. Cabot's next attack was on the twelve-hour day. "The Survey" published the facts concerning it and Mr. Cabot sent a letter to all his fellow stockholders about conditions, putting it clearly before them.

As I remember, the steel corporation was much concerned at his raising the twelve-hour day issue with the stockholders, and published letters favoring the twelve-hour day while Mr. Cabot published a number of letters from stockholders favoring its abandonment, even if it meant cutting dividends. Among these letters was mine, but the reform did not go through at this time. There was financial depression, Mr. Cabot died, and then came the war. Mr. Cabot, however, left a fund to be used in improving industrial conditions; some of this was used in investigations and only a short time ago the twelve-hour day was given up by the steel corporation.

I do not pretend in any way that what I did brought about any of these reforms. Undoubtedly all the corporations mentioned felt that they must make some changes, but I do feel that the protests of large stockholders had their influence, and that quicker action was taken than would otherwise have been the case. Stockholders are partners in a business in which they own shares; if they are indifferent to the conditions under which their employees work they are as culpable as if they were the actual employer, and while it is difficult to know the details of a business in which one owns stock, it is always possible to acquire this knowledge and to protest or approve at the annual meeting of the company to which all stockholders are bidden.

CHAPTER X

WOMAN'S CITY CLUB

When I was a little girl, I lived on Michigan Avenue near Twelfth Street. I often played in a yard on the corner of the street where a kind woman lived, who frequently invited me into her yard. One day my father, finding me playing there, was much shocked and forbade me going again, saying that the woman who lived there was a dangerous person—she wore her hair short, she had most radical opinions, and, worst of all, she was the President of a Woman's Club. That woman was Mrs. Kate Newell Doggett, who founded and was the president of The Fortnightly, and who was, I suppose, one of the most cultured women Chicago has ever known. I have often wondered whether, if my father had lived, his opinions would have changed as the opinions of all the world have changed, and if he would have been one of the committee of men who came, in later years, to Mrs. Wilmarth, a prominent and most lovely woman, and said to her, "We men have tried to better civic affairs but we have failed. Cannot you women do something?" Mrs. Wilmarth rose at once to the challenge and the Woman's City Club was born.

I attended the first meeting of this club, which was held in a room in the Chicago Public Library. I spoke, as well as many others. For awhile the new club, with a membership of about six hundred, met in the Library; then it rented some quarters in the School of Civics and Philanthropy, in the Tremont House Building on Dearborn and Lake Streets. The club was immediately divided into committees corresponding to the same committees of the city and county, such as City Finance, Garbage, Education, etc., and a competent woman was placed at the head of each committee. Later the quarters in the Tremont House became so cramped that the club moved into the Lakeview Building on Michigan Avenue. Here its membership dues were raised from one dollar to two dollars, and this change was considered so radical that the club lost seventeen hundred members, but soon gained them again. The club, under the competent directorship of Anna Nicholls and later Amelia Sears, aided by Grace Nicholls, grew in power and influence. Our membership increased and we moved into the new Stevens Building on Wabash Avenue.

When we moved into these new quarters we were on the seventeenth floor and we rented our rooms whenever possible. We were negotiating at one time with a clergyman concerning renting our lounge on Sunday afternoons. The clergyman finally gave up the idea because, owing to the height of the building, and the fact that so many millinery shops

MRS. BOWEN WITH SOME OF HER GRANDCHILDREN.

were to be seen from the elevator as it ascended, he did not believe he could take the room, as the attention of his congregation would be too much distracted by these frivolities.

The club occupied these quarters for eight years and has now moved into its new and beautiful rooms near the bridge on Michigan Avenue. To those of us who fifteen years ago met in the little dark room on Lake Street, it seems almost a miracle that the club has been able to finance itself and be such an important factor in the life of the city.

Shortly after the club moved to Michigan Avenue, it held a tremendous mass meeting to protest against a corrupt municipal administration. The Auditorium Theatre was crowded; women came two hours in advance in order to get seats. I was asked to preside at the meeting. First we read a Woman's Municipal Platform with twelve planks in it, including Civil Service, Department of Public Welfare, Telephone Franchise, Health, Schools, Housing, Public Recreation, Crime, Police, Non-Partisan City Elections, Municipal Voters' League, etc. There was a speaker for each plank. The meeting was a grand success; there were politicians and city office holders present in large numbers, and the club certainly registered itself as being an important organization with which city officials had to deal. Coming out from that meeting, one politician was heard to say, "And the trouble is, we cannot get those women."

Just after this meeting and before an aldermanic election, the club was anxious to find out how the various sitting aldermen had voted on the planks submitted for the Municipal Platform. It, therefore, sent its director to the City Council files and she put down (on what looked exactly like a baseball score) the way these aldermen had voted on various planks submitted at the meeting. She called it "The Aldermen's Batting Averages." The aldermen became very much interested in it and called frequently at the club rooms to look at their records. The club then published in the bulletin these batting averages, and advised its members to endorse such men as they felt had voted wisely on these various measures of public policy. I think it was owing to the big meeting in the Auditorium that I was made president of the club, because almost immediately after I was elected to this office. Just about this time I had a very serious operation and was ill for a year, so was obliged to resign, Miss Mary McDowell taking my place. After I recovered I was re-elected and was president of the club for ten years.

When I became president, the club had established itself and its commendation was sought on almost every question of public policy. Its representatives were invited to attend almost every public meeting and to sit in innumerable committees called by the city and county officials. The politicians were most anxious to know what stand the club was going to take on matters of public policy which came before the voters, and, before election, candidates sought its approval and asked permission to present their cause before its members.

The committees of the club were gradually increased until they numbered thirty-five, almost every committee corresponding with a department of the city or county. The chairmen of these committees kept in touch with what was going on in the municipality and, after bringing such matters before the board of directors of the club, carried their approval or their protest to the city or county.

The club then began to publish a small bulletin which carried information of club activities to all its members and which, before elections, published sketches of the candidates for all parties. It also gave advice on matters of public policy which were to come before the voters. The bulletin is now self-supporting, is widely read, not only by all members, but by men who often ask to see it before elections. Its articles have been copied in different papers all over the United States.

The club also instructs its members before election in the technique of voting. It has sample ballots to give away and it makes its members familiar with the questions which will come before them at the polls. When we consider that a voter is often given a ballot containing several hundred names of people about whom he or she has never heard, we realize how difficult it is for any voter, well informed or otherwise, to vote intelligently.

The club has held many meetings on the issues of the primaries and elections; at these meetings, candidates for office from all parties have made their plea for support. The club has been absolutely non-partisan and, while it has not invited representatives from every faction within a party, yet it has always invited a representative from each of the major parties.

At one time one of the committees of the club secured a list of candidates who were running for office, and sent club members with a questionnaire, to interview them so as to secure accurate information concerning their principles. These records were published in the bulletin. Some of these interviews were most illuminating to club members; one member said, "I can now visualize the candidates; they are not merely names. Even in the short talk with those allotted to me, I have formed my opinion and know whether I want to vote for them or not." One candidate told the interviewer that he was in politics for what he got out of it and this reply she set down on the questionnaire much to the annoyance of the candidate. Another candidate boasted to the interviewer that he never yet had been found out in any wrongdoing; this she also assured him would be reported to the club. Certainly this acquaintance with candidates for office has the advantage of bringing about a closer understanding between them and the electorate.

The club, many years ago, had reason to fear that the women police were not being used to the best advantage. Indeed they had heard rumors concerning the character of some of the women employed. They, therefore, had all the policewomen followed by an investigator and a report was made to the club concerning the manner in which these policewomen spent their time. The report revealed an astonishing amount of time wasted chatting in the corridors of the county and city building, sitting through sensational trials which had nothing to do with their work; attending luncheons at the houses of their friends, and going to afternoon teas, was found to be quite common among the policewomen at this time. There were also other charges of a graver nature.

The report was submitted to the supervisor of the policewomen and some steps were taken to give them more supervision and to remedy the evils of which the club complained.

Another piece of work done by this club a short time ago was most important. Some of the directors had reported that they felt that in many of the theatres the safety ordinances were being violated. The club then engaged a young woman as investigator; she visited about forty of the largest theatres in the city, serving as an usher in many of them. She made a most excellent report on each theatre, stating whether exits were locked, chairs placed in aisles, scenery not fireproof, fire apparatus not in order, etc. This report was sent by the club to the mayor who was most appreciative of it, and asked that the city officials in charge of the theatres be allowed an interview with the investigator. This was done; the report was most carefully gone over by the two people and the conditions complained of were rectified by the theatres. The investigation had no publicity, and yet, without doubt, was very valuable. Later the mayor asked if the same investigator would make a study of the hospitals of the city with reference to fire hazards.

At one time the city was in a financial dilemma and the Woman's City Club with Miss Sears as director, presented to the City Council a detailed report of these difficulties with some suggestions as to available remedies. This report caused quite a stir.

The Education Committee of the club repeatedly objected to certain actions of the Board of Education and because of their protest and those of other organizations, many conditions which were deleterious to the school children have been remedied.

The Young Woman's Auxiliary Committee was formed in connection with the club; six hundred young women organized into groups, became affiliated with it.

The club has ward leaders in the wards, also organizations in some of the county towns. The club holds ward leaders' luncheons once a month. I remember with great satisfaction what these ward leaders did during the war when they were appointed by the government fuel conservation chairmen for their districts. They then reported to the authorities the people in their neighborhoods who needed coal, and they were, therefore, able to conserve fuel and see that it was not obtained or hoarded by those who really did not need it.

A few years ago when there was great unemployment, the ward leaders undertook to work out the employment question in their wards. They tried to get householders to have their cellars whitewashed, yards cleaned, rooms calcimined, sidewalks repaired and then they reported these jobs to the State Employment Office so that men were sent to perform the work. The ward branches have in these and many other matters been most successful and are a very necessary part of the club.

The Civil Service Committee of the club took civil service off the shelf where it had become dusty and made it a live matter, full of human interest and great usefulness. These examinations were more often held by city and county committees and the authorities finally came to realize that the club was going to insist on civil service examinations whenever the law provided that they should be held.

The club is a busy, bustling place, putting out during the year several hundred pieces of printed matter and sending each month thousands of notices and letters. Occasionally it is reproached because it has so many well-to-do people as members; again it meets with abuse because it is too democratic and has too many working and professional people. The club is asked for all kinds of information and to do all kinds of work, from looking after the children of a mother while she does her shopping, to accompanying a woman to the divorce court in order that she may have a friend to stand by her.

The club has steadily followed the policy of coöperating with public officials to secure the enforcement of laws, for it believes that this is even more important than the making of new laws. This means a constant series of reports to officials of the violation of such laws as those concerning elections, building permits, health conditions, protection of children, vice repression, etc. Membership in the club is open to any woman who desires to use it as one means of expressing her interest in the community life of Chicago and Cook County. The club is asked to join all kinds of associations, from becoming a member of the Santo Domingo Independent Society to becoming a part of the International Rainbow Fairies Association, whatever that may be.

At one time when there was a judicial campaign for judges and there were ten Republicans and ten Democrats running for office, and it was a question of keeping the courts free from political domination, the club came out strongly for a coalition ticket;

it put out over ten thousand canned speeches, issued sixty thousand dodgers and four thousand letters. It served as a base for information and sent its speakers to all parts of the city.

The club conducted a question and answer column for many months in one of the Sunday papers, and in this way gave to the public information on subjects concerning which women should be well informed.

The club has a wonderful task before it. If it can continue to train women in the intelligent discharge of their duty as citizens; if it can consistently advocate such high standards for public service that the community may make them the test for its elected officials; if it can so fearlessly oppose corruption and expose graft that an outraged citizenship may be led to unite for better conditions in our community life, then indeed it will become the representative voice of women dedicated to civic righteousness.

CHAPTER XI

WOMEN IN WAR WORK

In February, 1917, a few days after the German Ambassador had been dismissed by President Wilson, Mrs. James Morrisson called together a number of women to consider what they should do if the country declared war. The meeting was a most interesting one; there were many pacifists present who did not want to take any immediate action, and there were others who wanted to form at once some kind of organization. A committee was finally appointed to investigate defense societies for women already organized in the East, and it was decided that the women should be called together again when this committee was ready to report. Mrs. George Isham was the chairman of this committee, and I was a member of it. Mrs. Ira Couch Wood, one of the most intelligent and brilliant women in Chicago, was asked to go East to look up the various defense organizations. After visiting a number of them in the East, Mrs. Wood presented a report of what was being done in the other large cities, and a meeting was held at my house to listen to the report. Mrs. Wood made some recommendations to the effect that an organization should be brought about in Illinois which would be a clearing house of women's activities and which would eliminate duplication of effort. This report was presented April, 1917, at Orchestra Hall with Mrs. Isham as temporary chairman. The women present who represented almost all of the organizations in the city, said they would be very glad to coöperate in any plan. A letter from Governor Lowden was read in which he stated that the plans suggested would fit in with the work of the State Council of Defense which was shortly to be appointed. A few days later, news came from Washington of the appointment of a Woman's Committee of the Council of National Defense, with Dr. Anna Howard Shaw as its chairman. The Illinois women then decided to form an Illinois division of this National Council of Defense, and I had the honor to be elected chairman as Mrs. Isham had died very suddenly. A few days later the State Council of Defense was appointed consisting of fifteen men, and I was appointed the only woman member of the board.

This council had been selected by Governor Lowden with great care and consisted of prominent men from Chicago and the state. I felt rather nervous about my first meeting with them. It was to be held at Springfield, and I was naturally anxious to make a good impression. On the way to Springfield there was a slight railroad accident, and the train arrived there at six in the morning while I was asleep. The porter roused me to say that I would have to get off at once, and I alighted on the platform with the other members of the council, clad in my outside coat, my shoes untied and my hair braided down my back. I had to drive up to the hotel in this costume.

Everything in the council was done in the most businesslike manner, but there was of course a tendency not to sympathize with the activities in which the women were engaged nor to care for the welfare plans for children which I advocated, although I tried to make the men feel that this was necessary as a war-time measure. I must say, however, that they were always extremely nice to me, and that I was given an entirely free hand in work among the women.

I admired Governor Lowden greatly. I felt that he was doing all in his power to win the war and that all his appointments were made with this end in view. In 1920 when he was a candidate for President, I campaigned for him in Chicago, but found to my surprise that the majority of the women were for General Wood or Mr. Hoover. This seemed to me rather ungrateful, as Governor Lowden made such a fine record during the war.

The women of the committee met at first in a little room in the Garland Building where the members sat around on soap boxes and wondered what they could do. They did not know exactly how to begin. We had previously sent on to Washington

Mrs. Wood's plan for the formation of an organization, and when we received the plan of the National Council of Defense we found that it was similar to the one sent by her.

In a few days we had outgrown the little room in the Garland Building, and we moved into a vacant store on East Madison Street. The women poured into this store in such numbers that we had to look about for larger quarters, and the State Council of Defense offered us rooms in the building which the Commonwealth Edison Company had offered rent free to it for the period of the war. Here in this building we had something like three floors, as our departments enlarged and new ones were formed. The State Council of Defense gave us the rooms rent free, light heat, telephones, the services of two stenographers, supplies and postage, approximating one thousand dollars a month.

Things moved quickly at this time. For example the woman at the information desk came to me one day and said, "I am asked for so much information about the war that I am simply swamped! Let me form an Information Department." I replied, "Go ahead." She secured a number of women who wrote well, took very much larger rooms, wrote to different parts of the country to know what was being done, obtained information from abroad, and put it out by the yard.

At another time my office was so filled with applicants for positions that we were obliged to start an employment department at once, and I was soon after threatened with arrest because I had not taken out a license.

The State Council of Defense was located in the same building, and I found it most convenient to go from my own organization to the floor on which it was located. The two worked in close coöperation, and I was very ably assisted in my work by the vice-chairman, Mrs. Frederick A. Dow, the women chairmen of departments, members at large of the Executive Committee, and by a committee representing almost every association of women in Chicago. During this time both the vice-chairman and I were in our offices from nine in the morning until sometimes six or seven at night, going through our correspondence, having any number of conferences and interviews, and speaking on all possible occasions to the full limit of our strength.

We did not even take time to leave the building for luncheon, it was sent down every day from my house, the coffee was made by one of the board members, and from twenty to thirty people would come in to my office every day to get their luncheon. This office was, at all times, free to the general public.

Our two organizations, the State Council of Defense and the Woman's Committee, National Council of Defense, Illinois Division, were combined under one set of officers, although we had two names.

I found these two names of great use on several occasions. At one time the legal adviser of the State Council of Defense gave it as his opinion that all the money raised by the women who were a part of the State Council should be put into the hands of the treasurer of the State Council and be requisitioned only by him, so then I said that all our money was raised under the name of the Woman's Committee, Illinois Division.

We had been told from Washington to prepare for a long war, and the first thing we did was to organize. We secured an organization secretary, and hung up in our office a big map of the State of Illinois. Whenever a county or village or city was organized a black pin was stuck in the map, and crowds of women visited the room from day to day to see how many pins the map had gathered. We built a most solid foundation. From Cairo to Galena, from Quincy to Paris, every city, town and township had added its unit to make up the most complete organization of women Illinois has ever attained; an organization including women of all classes, creeds, and nationalities, united in one democratic force under one standard, "Win the War."

We started the first registration in Chicago and then registered women all over the state. We registered for war work 700,000 women. There were, throughout the state, 2,136 local units, and we had 7,700 chairmen who directed the work of our 18 departments, our active workers numbering 326,333.

The registration cards of every city and town were kept by that unit and whenever we wanted workers for the governmental drives for which I would receive orders from Washington, I would call upon each unit to furnish us with volunteers. We were asked for people for the Exemption Boards, for nurses in the "flu" epidemics, student nurses for army and civilian hospitals, and for many other causes. Trained nurses were recruited from the registration cards, and we sent in the names of 1,200 applicants for the various hospitals. In Chicago alone we gave out 17,000 names of workers to various associations seeking volunteers. The women who registered offered every type of service from the stenographer who was working all day and offered to give two hours every evening to help win the war, to the little cripple who was confined to her bed and who said, sadly, that the only thing she could do was to train canary birds. Fortunately, we were able to give her carrier pigeons to train for army use, and in this she was most successful. There was another woman who registered that "She was willing and nervous, but that she could pray if necessary." There was the woman of wealth who offered her machine and her home with all of her employees for the use of wounded soldiers.

And there was the faithful and forehanded woman, who appeared one day clad in gold; gold tinsel dress, gold bonnet, gold muff, and even gold slippers. She said we were all going to be killed in the war, and she had on her resurrection dress ready to go to heaven at a moment's notice. From everywhere and from every sort of individual there came offers of assistance. No task seemed to be too great for anyone, no work too arduous. Every woman with whom we came in contact wanted to know what she could do to help, and did not mind performing any task, no matter how menial.

The Finance Department raised most of their money in a democratic way. Every woman who registered was charged ten cents for her registration fee, and this sum amounted to $70,000. In addition, the Finance Committee raised $100,000 partly from subscription and partly from business ventures. At one time, when the government was urging the use of potatoes instead of bread, the Finance Department put upon the streets of Chicago and in some of the towns throughout the state, bags of potato chips which they called Liberty Chips, and these chips, selling for five cents a bag, netted Chicago alone $7,000 in one day, not only advertising the fact that we must use potatoes, but bringing in a goodly amount of money. One of the hardest things I did during the war was to stand on La Salle Street and have my photograph taken as I wheeled a peddler's cart full of Liberty Chips up and down the block. In addition, about half a million dollars was raised by tag days for various war and other charities, and the finance committee sold $3,225,000 worth of Liberty Bonds.

The Speakers' Department, which, during the latter part of the war, consisted of both men and women, and did the work for the State Council of Defense, numbered 565 speakers. It held 2,408 meetings and reached 600,509 people, carrying its war message to even the most remote towns in the state. Some of the requests for speakers were, of course, most absurd. One club wrote asking us to send at once an atrocity who would tell war stories set to music; but on the whole the demand was genuine, and it was solely needed. At one meeting on the subject of thrift and war saving stamps—and the meeting was composed of educated and intelligent people—the idea seemed to be that war saving stamps and thrift stamps were much like the Red Cross tuberculosis stamps, and must be pasted on the outside of letters. At another meeting where the subject was Liberty Bonds, a foreign woman rose and said "she didn't think it was right for the government to put out those bonds. They were the kind her old man always used when he wanted to get out of jail, and she didn't think the government ought to make it any easier for him and any harder for her."

The Speakers' Bureau had been told to be quick to seize opportunities to get the subject before the people. One of the speakers, a very forceful woman, went to the southern part of the state at the time of the influenza epidemic. She wrote back to the chief of her department in Chicago saying that there had been a ban upon meetings—that none could be held—there were only funerals. Her chief, perhaps rather lightly, responded, "Better go to the funerals." The speaker was a literal person, and she went to the first large funeral. The church was full, and after the mourners had left the church she stood up and in a commanding voice said, "Stop! Listen! I have a message from the government!" They naturally stopped and listened. She gave a message on the subject of child welfare, and immediately formed a Child Welfare League in that town.

We had some women who were making short speeches and we had had some complaints that they were not doing it very well, so I asked these women to prepare their speeches and make them to me, and I really felt sorry for them, as they would come into my office and have to make their speeches (to which I must say I paid very little attention as I was usually occupied), and it was a hard thing for them to do.

We were very near the offices of the American Protective League, a branch of the Bureau of Secret Service, and found at one time that our information desk had a spy at it, evidently put there by German sympathizers to find out what was going on. I had to dismiss her and it was an extremely disagreeeable job.

I have told of the necessity of forming an employment department. This department proved to be most useful. It found positions for 2,205 women who reported back that they had taken the positions to which they were sent. Probably the number was much larger, but many did not report back. Most of these women were over forty years of age, and utterly untrained. As I would go into the waiting room of the Employment Department I was always struck with the fact that most of these women were wearing fur coats, and that the majority of them had to supplement their income because the bread-winners were at the war, although a few, I regret to say, wanted positions of responsibility with no work. One woman said "she would like to open the mail of the association, and be responsible for its keys." Some of them felt that they knew all about children and they wanted positions to teach children, their reasons being no better than that of the Irish woman who had borne ten children and lost nine, and, therefore, thought she knew all about them.

We soon found that we had to have some kind of training for these women, and classes of instruction were started, not only in Chicago, but in sixty-five other cities throughout the state, and ninety courses were offered where women could get training which would enable them to take some kind of clerical position. There were courses in filing, indexing, telegraphy, stenography, typing, bookkeeping, signaling, teaching, housekeeping, and so on. These classes were conducted almost without expense, as the positions of teachers were taken by women or men incapacitated for service who had had previous experience in their own lines. For example, we found many married women who had been telegraphers, and who instructed other women in that work. In this connection it was found necessary to establish a mending shop for the older women, as many of them were over seventy years old and too feeble to take regular positions. This shop proved to be very successful, and after the war it was taken over by the Chicago Woman's Club, and is now, I believe, self-supporting.

These were busy days for me. My two boys were over seas, one a captain at the front, fighting in the trenches, the other a lieutenant in the navy, a torpedo officer on a destroyer. I was most anxious about them, but felt that the harder every one worked the sooner the war would be won.

I had to meet once a week always with the State Council of Defense, and many times there were extra committee meetings. One part of my work with the State Council was reporting all the saloons which were selling liquor to the soldiers and sailors. I used for my investigators in this instance officers of the Juvenile Protective Association. With the chairman of the State Council of Defense, Mr. Insull, I had frequent meetings with the owners of saloons or cafés, and I may say these meetings were almost always disagreeable, but they certainly brought about some results.

The State Council of Defense did a magnificent piece of work all over the state. Its activities had largely to do with questions concerning military matters, finances, crops, business, etc., while the women's work had more to do with the women and children, and with the practical details of the home.

The Child Welfare Department of the Woman's Committee was maintained and financed by the Elizabeth McCormick Memorial Fund. It weighed and measured 325,000 children and instructed the parents as to their proper care. This department by its wonderful work succeeded in arousing the whole state to the necessity of conserving its children. Even the school boys became excited on the subject, and one boy wrote a composition in which he said, "Now that we are at war, it is everybody's duty to have a baby and to save it."

This department recommended the establishment of child welfare centers, the employment of community nurses, the extension of medical inspection in the schools, and the education of mothers concerning the care of their children.

During the war I often received orders from Washington to call upon the women of the state to practice conservation and our Conservation Department gave demonstrations in almost every town and city in the state concerning substitutes for flour and sugar, the remaking of clothes, the necessity for the elimination of waste. In Chicago, we had these demonstrations in vacant shops, in department stores and in settlements, and finally, when we found that we were not reaching the foreign population, we fitted up a motor van and portable kitchen, and gave our demonstrations from this van on the street corners in the foreign parts of the city. We estimated that by this we reached hundreds of thousands of women who tasted our corn bread and took away our little pamphlets with the recipes for making bread out of materials other than white flour.

We tried to reach the girls of the state, and we enrolled in Chicago 12,000 of them in what we called Patriotic Leagues, and we established a Social Hygiene Department which gave them instructions necessary to their well-being. The chairman of this department did her work so well and scientifically that she was made head of the Woman's Division of the State Department of Health under the title of Supervisor of Education for Women. She and members of her department went to many of the factories in the city and talked to the girls during their luncheon hour, so that in this way she reached something like 54,000 girls who worked in industrial establishments.

The Food Production Department immensely stimulated the raising of crops throughout the state. I advocated what were called war gardens, and something like 90,000 of these war gardens were reported. The Woman's Committee assumed the responsibility and management of a farm at Libertyville, Illinois, and there it trained young women in agricultural and dairying pursuits. It received over a thousand applications from girls who were interested in this subject, and turned out seventy-six young farmers.

Many of us had found that we had great difficulty with our cooks; they would not be economical; some of them felt that it was not at all necessary to save on white flour, sugar or any of the materials which, during the war, we were asked to conserve. We then decided to hold a meeting at the Auditorium Theatre exclusively for the cooks of the city. All cooks were invited, the chef of the Sherman House presiding. Patriotic speeches were made concerning the necessity of conserving certain foods, etc. The effect of this meeting was most gratifying. Cooks, after all, are as patriotic as anyone else, and when the part they could play in the conservation of food was put before them, they arose to the occasion and did their very best to use the substitutes recommended by the State Council of Defense.

The Information Department with its 500 representatives supplied speakers, schools, clubs and libraries with up-to-date material about the war, and it sent out what we called canned speeches all through the state. At one time it distributed 143,000 pamphlets to be used in the high schools in Chicago.

Our Publicity Department sent a news letter throughout the state every week. It published three War Time Recipe Books; it conducted a "Do Without" club, and also a candy kitchen from which it sold candy made without sugar.

The Social Welfare Department made connection between 1,516 volunteers and social agencies, and it provided wool for the shut-ins in hospitals, insane asylums, old people's homes, and prisons, where the inmates felt for the first time that they were doing their bit toward winning the war. It was estimated that this department saved agencies $100,000, which would otherwise have been paid to employees.

The Allied Relief Department raised an enormous sum and sent to Europe large quantities of hospital supplies, garments and kits, and adopted 8,844 fatherless children.

For nearly two years the women of Illinois did their best. Some of them lost their husbands and sons, others heard that their loved ones were missing. There was doubt and uncertainty and always anxiety and the horror of the war. Then came the Armistice, we heard in Chicago a report that it had been signed previous to the real event. My first news of it came through one of the women on my committee who burst into my office, and, throwing her arms around my neck, said, "Your boys are coming back to you but mine rest in France." Other members of the committee then rushed in, full of the joyful news. There was music from outside, we threw open the windows, the street was full of people, the air heavy with bits of paper thrown from scrap baskets; some one had moved a piano to the middle of the street, and a man was playing "Onward Christian Soldiers," suddenly the whole crowd began to sing the national anthem, and, in our office we all stood at attention, as had been our custom during the war. Underneath my window my attention was attracted to a dozen chefs, from some nearby hotel kitchen, who had left their stoves and in white caps and jackets were marching in an orderly manner singing the Marseillaise, holding over their right shoulders long bunches of celery, apparently the only thing they could grab in their hurried exit.

I went at once to a big meeting in the La Salle Hotel where I was presiding and, much to my surprise, almost broke down as I tried to tell the audience what it meant to the world to see the end of the war. To my bitter disappointment the speaker of the day, a newspaperman, then arose and announced that he had just received a telegram saying the Armistice had not yet been signed; however, three days later, when peace was consummated every man, woman and child in the city was on the streets, such shouting, such singing, such a day of jubilation, the world perhaps has never seen. It was a wild day, but one which no one will ever forget.

At the beginning of the war, or rather, soon after the state had been organized, I gave a large dinner at the Morrison Hotel to 1,000 of my chairmen who came up to this dinner. It was a most inspiring occasion. We had our song books at every plate, and sang war songs, and some of the most spirited speeches on winning the war that I have ever heard were made at that time. Later on, when the war was over, I gave another dinner at this same place to these chairmen, and made then my final report on the work which had been accomplished. As the Woman's Committee had quite a large sum of money left in its treasury, we continued our work for another year, trying to establish community centers throughout the state. Something like fifty of these centers were established, but I doubt very much if they have been permanent. The Woman's Committee was so well organized and its departments and sub-committees were so efficient that it seemed a pity to give up the work. We soon found, however, that when the war urge was over, interest subsided. I was forcibly struck by this one day. It had been my habit whenever an order came from Washington and a letter had to go out to our chairmen throughout the state, to have one of the departments telephone for volunteers, and we could always get with a few hours' notice 200 volunteers in an evening at the office to direct envelopes. Just after the war was over, I issued such a call, and the chairman of that department came down to tell me, almost with tears in her eyes, that she could only get two people to respond!

Of course, during the war we were all looking in our minds' eye at the shell-torn battlefields of France, the ruined villages, the desolate homes, the long, dusty roads filled with artillery wagons, motors, guns, cannons, ambulances, and all the paraphernalia of war and that endless procession of khaki-clad men who had crossed the seas to fight for the greatest cause for which any nation ever fought, and we know now that those boys of ours, with a smile on their lips and the spirit of the Crusader in their hearts, went into the fight just at the crucial moment, and by the sheer weight of their will to win turned the tide and pushed back the foe. Most of these men, thank God, came back to us, but many of them sleep in France. All honor to them and to the brave and noble dead of our Allies, with whom the fields of France are sown. "They found their lives by losing them. They forgot themselves, but they saved the world!"

These men who fought so nobly were fighting for Democracy, but we will never have a real democracy in this country—that democracy of which we caught just a glimpse during the war when we were brought together by a common danger and a common sympathy—until we once more continuously work together for the good of our community—until we learn to reverence, not the aristocracy of wealth and position, but the aristocracy of service—until we can assure to every citizen of this great Republic equal opportunities for health, for education, for work, for decent living, for love, and for happiness.

It will be remembered that soon after the war the prices of all commodities were extremely high. The people of the United States seemed to have an orgy of spending. They were tired from the war, tired of making sacrifices and economizing. They threw off all caution, drew upon their savings and spent lavishly. Working men wore twenty dollar silk shirts and working girls eight hundred dollar fur coats bought upon the instalment plan and worn out before payment was completed. The government, in an effort to bring down the high cost of living, appointed Fair Price Commissioners in every state, with the idea that they could arrive at a conclusion concerning just charges for food, clothes and all commodities, and publish the prices in the daily press. I was appointed by the Department of Justice the Woman Fair Price Commissioner for Illinois. Colonel A. A. Sprague had already been appointed to represent the men, while I was to do the work among the women. We had offices together in the Federal Building, and I was much impressed—or unimpressed—by the manner in which buildings are managed where the government is the owner. Never have I seen such crowded elevators or such poor service. Our room was never well cleaned, it had one rather disreputable washroom in it used by both men and women, the windows were so seldom washed that they were almost opaque with the dirt. It was, on the whole, rather an uncomfortable experience, but one attended by many amusing incidents. The government gave me an executive secretary, several stenographers, and told me to engage anyone I pleased for the work. Every morning from six to a dozen reporters surrounded my desk to find out my plans for the day. I found it, to tell the truth, very difficult, not only to make daily plans, but to make any at all. If a rabbit had been set down in a coal mine and told to mine coal every day, he couldn't have been more ignorant than I was how to proceed. I began by calling together the women of my Executive Committee who had worked with me during the war, and we started a campaign of education throughout the state, using many of the same chairmen who had worked for us during the war. Never have I received so much advice on how to manage any organization as I did about the Fair Price Commission. There were always several people waiting to see me to tell me how to proceed. One day a man deposited upon my desk a loaf of bread made out of some strange material, and told me that if all the world ate this bread they not only would be well and happy, but prosperous. Another man once brought me a worn-out old shoe. He showed with great pride the sole in this shoe which he had invented, and he assured me that if every citizen of Chicago wore these soles they would be so lifted up from the earth and brought so near heaven that the price of food would quickly be reduced.

I was obliged to engage a woman for publicity purposes alone in order to keep not only the newspapers but the government satisfied that the women were doing something. We sent through the state a woman to talk on budgets, and we secured from the best informed people in the country budgets for working men with incomes varying from one to five thousand dollars. We induced some of the big retail stores on State Street to give up one window to low priced apparel. One large store, after trying this window for a week with women's dresses and shoes marked at most reasonable prices, told me that it was not worth while for them to keep up the window any longer, as not one single person had come into that department to ask to look at these goods. On the other hand, another store reported that women with shawls over their heads were buying banquet lamps and feather fans, and that the perfume counter was besieged by girls who wanted, not the best perfumes, but the most expensive. I found that I had to be very careful lest in advertising a certain commodity of any kind I was advertising that particular firm. I remember one time I was asked to publish the fact that a certain food was to be had very cheaply, and to advise the public to purchase it. It seemed to me very wise and reasonable, but I managed to get some information on the subject and found to my horror that the firm who wanted me to advertise this food had an immense quantity of it on hand, and wanted me to advertise it simply to clean their shelves.

I had looked forward with much pleasure to the visit of the woman who had been placed by the Department of Justice at the head of the women's work of the nation in reducing the cost of living. She came to visit me on her arrival in Chicago, and I found to my great disappointment that she was very young—perhaps not over twenty-two years of age—that she had had no experience in this line of work, and had very few suggestions to make concerning it.

If in any way I was able, for example, to lower the price of eggs in Chicago I immediately was called upon by dozens of farmers who asked me if I had ever run a farm, and if I knew how much food was required and how much attention and coaxing necessary to get hens to lay eggs. If by any chance the price of eggs went up, I received dozens of almost threatening letters from housewives who told me that I had an interest in the egg business, and was profiting by the rise.

We held many lectures at the Federal Building in a vacant court room next to our quarters. From this court room we were sometimes summarily expelled by an irate judge who had no use for women's dabbling in economics. Notwithstanding, we managed to give a great many lectures by experts on how to purchase materials, how to make clothes, how to buy inexpensive and nourishing food. In this connection, I remember with much amusement a government official who came to us to talk on the best and cheapest fish procurable in Chicago. He mentioned four kinds and advised their purchase. I had never heard of any of them, but thought this was due to my ignorance. However, after a tour of the fish markets of the city, we found that not a single one of these fish was obtainable, and we, therefore, felt that in listening to the lecture of this learned fish man we had somewhat wasted our time.

We did not consider that department of the government with which we had to deal extremely businesslike. Although we had been told to engage a force of clerks, we found great difficulty in getting their salaries. Many times Colonel Sprague and I advanced money for our stenographers, and these self-respecting young women did not like to take money in this way, and very often left us. After a time I found it very difficult to get any money, and I was not allowed enough to start the educational campaign for economy which I had planned. I afterwards found out that I had been given this appointment on the supposition that I was a Democrat, and when it was later found that I was a good Republican there was no effort made to make things easy for me. Therefore, I resigned, not knowing whether I had accomplished anything or not, but hoping that the educational campaign for thrift and economy which our women had made throughout the state would, in the long run, count for something.

CHAPTER XII

WOMEN IN PUBLIC AFFAIRS

When the Nineteenth Amendment of the Constitution of the United States was passed and women were given the franchise, there was much discussion as to whether the women's votes would only duplicate the number of ballots cast on election day or whether they would act independently of the men of their household and register their own approval or disapproval of the candidates seeking election. That women were expected to reflect the sentiment of the men of their families was perhaps only natural and no doubt many a woman has followed humbly in the footsteps of her father or husband. However, many of the leading women's organizations of the country immediately instituted classes in citizenship and gave instructions on the current political questions of the day. The men's political organizations throughout the country immediately sought leading women to serve on their factional committees. These women were supposed to lend their leadership to strengthen the men's organizations, but they were never to lose sight of the fact that they were to do the men's bidding. They sat in the caucuses but they had no voice in the selection of candidates.

It took the women of Chicago about two years to realize this situation, and the fact that every woman is vitally concerned in government, since it touches almost every relationship of her daily life through officials whom she should help to choose; therefore, in June, 1921, a group of eight representative Chicago women met in a small office in the Fine Arts Building and decided to form a Republican Woman's Club which should be independent of factional differences. These women worked unceasingly through that summer, forming committees, raising funds, interesting women in politics, etc., and the following September they called a meeting of the Republican women in Chicago, at the Congress Hotel; a charter was applied for, a constitution and by-laws adopted, officers elected, and the Woman's Roosevelt Republican Club was officially launched as the first independent Republican woman's club in Illinois.

I joined this club soon after it was started, as I had begun to feel from my long experience with various organizations that if we could get good and honest men into public office they could do more to bring about the reforms women had wanted to accomplish than all the reform organizations in the city, and I, therefore, determined to devote a good deal of my time to politics, not in the usual acceptance of the word, but because I considered politics the shortest road to good government, and I was most anxious to see what women could do. The Roosevelt Club proved to be extremely independent. It is opposed to boss rule, and to the evils of the spoils system. It has frequently demonstrated its independence by refusing to endorse, in city, county or state elections, men of whom it could not approve. The club offers women the opportunity to organize along party lines and to take an active part in the choice of candidates in the party primaries. It instructs women in the technique of voting, and it holds, from time to time, meetings addressed by leaders of the Republican party. It has most delightful club rooms on Michigan Avenue where I have an office, and here it holds round-table discussions and lectures on most of the current political matters of the day. I served as vice-president of this club for two or three years, and then was elected president, which position I am still filling. I do not like politics. It is very difficult for me to compromise. There have been many times when the board of directors of the club have not known what to do. One of those instances was when we wanted to put a fine woman in as one of the judges of the Circuit Court. We visited the party factional leaders who were then in power, and they agreed to put the name of this woman on the ticket provided that we would endorse the other judges who were also on the ticket. The majority of these judges were good. A few did not meet our standards, and we took a long time before finally deciding that we would endorse the whole ticket, which was later elected. It is very difficult to make decisions in these matters. If in this case we had refused to endorse the whole ticket because there were a few poor men upon it, then our candidate would not have been put upon the ticket, and would have had no chance of election.

I was very much impressed at this time with the power of an organized body. I had been a member of a committee representing a large number of the women's clubs in Chicago and we had been as a committee to visit some of the factional leaders to request that some women candidates be put on the ticket for County Commissioners. These men were fairly polite to us, telling us to go home and not think anything more about the matter—that when they were ready they would call us in for consultation. One of them even tapped me on the shoulder and said, "Don't think about it again. We will be sure to put you on some committee!" We went home, and it was about this time that the Woman's Roosevelt Club was organized. Soon afterward, I was put upon a committee to go again to these factional leaders and demand that they put some women candidates on the county ticket. We went representing a party organization. They did not receive us perhaps quite as politely as the first time, but after we had told them the club which we represented, that our membership was a large one, that we had branches in the wards and in the various towns of Cook County, they asked the question: "Whom do you want put on the ticket?" We gave the names of two women, to which they acquiesced, and these women, Miss Helen Bennett and Mrs. George R. Dean, made a most excellent campaign, and ran very high on their ticket, but unfortunately it was a Democratic year, and the Republican ticket was not elected. This shows, I think, quite conclusively that a body of women, organized along party lines, can do much more than an unorganized body, and we never told those politicians that the Roosevelt Club, although it did have branches in the wards and county towns, had then altogether only three hundred members. Now, however, its membership numbers many thousands.

I can remember the club endorsing two or three men for public office and then finding out just before election that they were apparently seeking the support of a mayor of whom we did not approve. The Executive Committee of the Roosevelt Club sat late that evening, wondering what they would do. They were organized to fight our corrupt municipal administration, and they could not bear to think that they were endorsing anyone who was in any way affiliated with the officials who composed this administration. Late that night the club sent two of its members to the newspaper offices and these newspapers bore the next morning the news that the club had withdrawn its endorsement of certain candidates. We were almost afraid that it might ruin the club, but on the whole it was an exhibition of courage, and from that time on the club increased in membership and in influence.

About this time there was to be a primary for mayoralty candidates. I sat often with a Committee of men and women who were to choose a candidate. There was not much difficulty in selecting men who would make admirable mayors, but the obstacle encountered was the fact that these men would not consent to allow their names to be used as candidates. While this committee was sitting and its deliberations were being closely watched by the politicians, the board of the Woman's Roosevelt Club, at a time when I was not present, met with the head of one of the factions of the Republican party. He asked the board of the Roosevelt Club for suggestions for mayor, when one of my good friends said that she had a person to suggest who would combine all the qualities necessary for a mayor. After he had listened eagerly to her recommendations of the perfect person he asked the name, and she said, "Mrs. Joseph T. Bowen!" All the members of the board present told me that it was funny to watch his face. First he looked incredulous; then he seemed to think it was the best joke in the world, but as he pondered on it he began to think that perhaps it wasn't such a bad idea. On leaving the meeting he said he would confer with his associate, who was at the head of another faction of the party, and would give his opinion later.

That very afternoon, or perhaps it was the next day, I was at a very important meeting and was told that these gentlemen wished to see me. I had to tell them that they would have to wait if they wanted me, and I regret to say that I kept them waiting for over an hour. When I went in to see them they both told me that my name had been suggested as candidate for mayor, and they offered me the support of their organizations. I thanked them and said I would take the matter under consideration, but I asked why they wanted a woman. I said: "I know you really don't want me because you think I would be a good mayor. There must be some reason why you are willing to offer your support to a woman." The reply, as near as I can remember it, comprised: First, to run a woman for mayor of a large city like Chicago would make good publicity, and as all the women would probably vote for me (I didn't contradict him, but I wasn't at all sure of it) that I would poll a very large vote. Second, whoever was put up might be accused of belonging to the Ku Klux Klan, and there was no possibility that I could be charged with being a member of it. Third, it was taken for granted that I wouldn't want to form a political machine, and that would be an advantage. We then parted. I had no idea whatever of running for mayor. Had I been twenty years younger I would have liked to try it. Not that I would have been elected, but I would have liked the campaigning, the publicity which I could have for the objects in which I was interested, and possibly I could have put up a municipal program and set up some standards which would have been of use to the rival candidate. After consultation with some of my men friends and with the women with whom I was most closely connected, I determined not to give an answer at once in the hope that the party would put up a good candidate on the Republican ticket rather than have a woman, and I had the feeling that if I withheld my decision they would do much to get a good person. We women were right in our surmise. While the newspapers said nothing against me, and all were good enough to acknowledge that I was capable, etc., they all insisted that no woman should be elected mayor of so large a city as Chicago, and they urged every committee that was working on the subject to produce a good candidate. When the committee on which I was sitting had decided on Mr. Arthur Lueder to head the Republican party I gave my reply, which was that I did not care to run, but we women always felt that we had contributed a little to putting up a good Democratic candidate, Mr. Dever, as well as the Republican candidate, Mr. Lueder.

About this time I was given a degree of Master of Arts at Knox College, Galesburg, Illinois. This college has turned out many famous men, and I considered it a great honor to receive a degree from it. I shall never forget the beautiful day when we

From drawing by George Davis. Published by Rufus Blanchard.

CHICAGO IN 1832.

marched across the college campus in cap and gown, past the stately old college buildings covered with ivy and into a large church where the degrees were conferred. It was a most delightful experience, and one which made me feel most unworthy of the honor. My education was finished at a very early age, and it was a great pleasure to feel that what I had been able to do had attracted enough attention to make college trustees feel that I deserved a degree.

On the whole, I was as busy as any one person could well be. I took care of my own business and made my own investments. I was connected with so many organizations and had so many meetings and speeches to make that I hardly had any time to myself. One day in the fall of 1924 I noticed that my mail was a large one, and just for curiosity, as I opened every letter, I had my secretary take down the contents of it. I found that in this one mail I had seventy requests either to make contributions, to buy, to sell, or to attend meetings. The following list at least illustrates the growing complexity of life in a modern city. I was asked:

To buy stock in a certain trust company.
To entertain a prominent woman.
To attend a church dancing party.
To go into business in a cleaning and dyeing company.
To attend a course of lectures on the theatre.
To buy bonds of a foreign company.
To visit and give to a prominent hospital.
To go to a series of concerts.
To build a new hospital.

To join the "Big Tree League of California."
To subscribe to a public health magazine.
To write a letter of condolence to the family of a public official.
To found a school of music.
To subscribe to a monthly review on music.
To join an association of railroad owners.
To go on a trip around the world.
To subscribe to a journal of health.
To buy lingerie of a new firm.
To use my name in an advertisement for political purposes.
To advance some money for a worthy cause.
To vote the straight Republican ticket.
To join a music association.
To patronize a certain beauty parlor.
To buy my Christmas presents at a certain jewelry store.
To vote the Democratic ticket.
To patronize a certain chiropodist.
To give a subscription for a settlement.
To attend a series of lectures on wood prints.
To attend a luncheon on social service.
To send my autograph for certain purposes.
To become a subscriber to an Eastern paper.
To go on a cruise on the Seven Seas.
To join a certain Chicago club.
To invest my funds in a disreputable concern.
To make an investment in a certain company.
To send my signature for business purposes.
To patronize a bucket shop.
To give a subscription to the Salvation Army.
To attend an exhibition at the Drake Hotel.
To put all my savings in a magazine of fashion.
To be Chairman of a large Committee about to be formed.

To buy a book on etiquette.
To buy my Christmas linens of a New York firm
To attend two public luncheons.
To send a check to a children's charity.
To send a check for a Presbyterian church.
To visit a famous hotel in the South.
To buy my diamonds at a New York jewelers.
To purchase my linens at a New York linen store.
To buy my opera coats at a certain store.
To buy my tea gowns at a certain store.
To send my old clothes to a re-sale shop.
To give to a Presbyterian Home.
To buy old carpets at a certain shop.
To attend a luncheon and hear a celebrated speaker.
To buy clothing for myself and family at a certain store.
To use my name on a Republican advertisement.
To vote for Governor Small on the ground of his good service.
To become vice-president of a large political club.
To give a talk over the radio.
To preside at a political meeting.
To hold a meeting concerning a matter of public policy.
To patronize a detective agency.
To accept as a gift a suit of underwear and a pair of silk stockings.
To give my opinion on some candidates for re-election.
To support a string quartette.
To buy some old prints.
To endorse three separate candidates for the same office for election.
To order some photographs.

About this time there had been a demand from the women to have some women on the Republican National Committee, and in the summer of 1924 I was appointed Associate Republican National Committeewoman from Illinois. I remember I had a very nice letter from Mrs. Coolidge expressing her pleasure at my appointment and at the fact that women were to be organized. I should have been at the Republican National Convention held in Cleveland in 1924, but unfortunately I was ill at that time and could not attend. The women there made a fight for the fifty-fifty rule, which allowed an equal representation of women on the Republican National Committee. Thanks to the efforts of Senator Pepper, Mrs. Medill McCormick, Mrs. George R. Dean, and many others, the fight was a success, and the fifty-fifty rule went into effect, Mrs. Medill McCormick then being elected by the Illinois delegation as the Republican Committeewoman from Illinois.

Shortly after the Woman's Roosevelt Republican Club was organized, a great effort was made to organize the Republican women of the state, with local clubs in every town and city. Mrs. George R. Dean heads this organization, and has something like ninety clubs organized throughout the state. I am one of the vice-presidents of this organization, the Roosevelt Club being one of its members. The two organizations coöperate most closely, the Roosevelt Club doing the work for Chicago and the other clubs for the state. The Illinois clubs hold a convention once a year, a most dignified gathering, and I am sure many of the men politicians, if they were present at these deliberations, would feel that the women were a great power with which they must reckon.

We have always found that the hardest thing in the world is to hold together a political organization when there is no need for immediate action. Just before an election is no time to organize, so that, between elections, we must secure members, and then, when the time comes, the machine, perfectly oiled, may be set in motion. If we live under the protection of the greatest nation in the world, we should at least be cognizant of the functioning of that government and how it affects us as individuals. We all want good government, but we must not forget that all the benefits of good government depend upon the officials whom we select and whose duties we define. No government can rise higher in its standards and conceptions than the aggregate ideals of the individual voters. Women, having won suffrage, have deprived themselves of the privilege of grumbling about the government. We are now, as we never were before, The People. We are The Government, and if it fails to function as it should, then it is we who are responsible.

It is very difficult always to finance political clubs. One day a committee was appointed by the president of the Illinois Women's Republican Clubs to devise means to raise money. Miss Helen Bennett, one of the directors of the Woman's Roosevelt Republican Club, suggested that we hold a World's Fair, and that we use the proceeds of this fair for financing the Republican women. This idea was accepted by the women, a board of directors was formed, called The Women's World's Fair, Inc., and I was elected president. The fair was held in April, 1925, and was a great success, netting something like $40,000 for the women. In 1926 the fair is again to be held with the Juvenile Protective Association as its beneficiary. The fair was a revelation of the multiplicity of occupations in which women had scored successes, and it might have been called a vocational show, as it gave evidence of so many occupations and professions open to women. The fair was opened over the radio by a speech made by President Coolidge, who commended the women for what they had done, and he especially noted the fact that when the doors of the fair were opened there was enough money in the treasury to pay all the bills contracted. Mrs. Coolidge also pressed the button which opened the fair, and it was closed by Vice-President Dawes. The United States Government sent exhibits from its various departments, women artists showed their best work in the art gallery, women in all professions and trades and women in business gave their experience to the crowds of high school girls who attended in large groups. Department stores, railroad companies, and other corporations made exhibits, while the social welfare agencies took this opportunity to place before the public a record of what they were doing to educate people to relieve suffering, to improve civic matters and to put through all the other social-work activities which are so much needed by every great city. The official program of the fair was produced entirely by women, illustrated by a woman, and printed by a woman. Many important people attended the fair, including women college presidents, a woman federal judge, and the woman Governor of Wyoming. As I was president of the fair, I gave a great deal of time to it, and during the week it was open I was at it constantly in the information booth, where I met people and talked with them on every conceivable topic. One rather pathetic thing showed, I think, the confidence which a young woman had once inspired. We were having a luncheon for famous women—a luncheon which proved such a success that although we seated seven hundred people, more than nine hundred were turned away. The day before the luncheon an old man came to me and said: "Can you tell me where I will find Jenny Jones?" I said: "No, who is she? Is she exhibiting here?" He said: "I don't know." I asked if Jones was her married name. He said she was married, but he had forgotten the man's name. He had not seen Jenny for forty years, but she was such a smart girl and such a good one when he knew her so long ago in a little Indiana town where they both lived, that he felt sure she must have become famous, and so he had come up to the city to find her. At the Famous Women's Luncheon the next day I wanted to pay a tribute to the women who did not sit at the speakers' table, and who perhaps were famous in a way that we did not know, and I told this story, which had happily come to me the day before.

Great expositions of this kind are sometimes wearisome for people who have to go to them frequently, but they have a great educational value, and this Woman's World's Fair at least showed the business men of the city that women could undertake a great enterprise of this kind and put it through successfully, and it also had its value in showing women by practical demonstrations the number of occupations open to them and the success which they might attain in any one of these occupations or professions. I had a most interesting time at the fair with General Dawes, Vice-President of the United States, who went with me through the fair and who made a speech over the radio. I found Governor Nellie Ross of Wyoming a most charming woman, as well as a wise politician. She made a great impression upon everyone she met, and when such women are elected to office and fill their positions creditably it is a great encouragement to women who are striving to put good people into elected positions of trust.

I have served on many other organizations about which I have said nothing. One of these is the Chicago Council of Social Agencies, an organization which has tried to gather together all the welfare associations of the city, and to combine them by groups in order that duplication of effort might be avoided, and their work done more effectively. I also served for something like twelve years on the Committee of Fifteen, which at one time did most excellent work in eliminating vice. I was for about two years on the Birth Control League, and for a year on the Illinois Training School for Nurses. I am a member of the Executive Committee of the Foreign Language Information Service; I was for many years on the League to Enforce Peace, the Needlework Guild, the Lower North Community Council and many other organizations, all of which helped, I hope, in the improvement and the enlargement of life in Chicago.

In my childhood I frequently attended exhibitions given at the old Exposition Building on Michigan Avenue, where we went to hear the Thomas Concerts and drink beer at little tables; where in the winter time we girls played tennis on a sawdust floor of the cold, unlighted building. Now the Art Institute, a center of art for this part of the country, stands where this building stood, and just outside the beautiful Fountain of the Great Lakes pours its waters lavishly, symbolizing Chicago at the foot of the great chain. Farther down in Grant Park, where I once fell into the water, stands the wonderful Field Museum of Natural History, crowded every day with hundreds of people; across from the Art Institute is Orchestra Hall, housing the Chicago Symphony Orchestra, the fame of which has gone throughout the world, demonstrating that Chicago is a center for the Arts as well as for Commerce.

As I close this book I am looking from the window of my office in the London Guarantee Building, on the very site of Fort Dearborn. I look from one window up the Chicago River, past the new Wacker Drive, once South Water Street, where my grandfather was a commission merchant. The river, with its busy docks, is filled with boats and crossed by many bridges; after serving early Chicago almost as a sewer, it has been restored to its early purity by the great canal, and no longer placidly flows toward the prairie or toward the lake as the rainfall dictates.

Not far along this drive was once a little hotel kept by my great-uncle, where travelers were made welcome and given the best the little inn could afford.

A short distance south of the Wacker Drive, my father sat in the office of his bank and made his first loans to the merchants who were even then building their grain elevators and establishing a center for the meat industry of the world.

I look out another window across the sparkling waters of Lake Michigan and up Michigan Boulevard where the great Wrigley Building stands, and the beautiful *Tribune* structure lifts its tower toward heaven.

I also look at the Kirk Building where stood the home of the first white man in Chicago, John Kinzie, my grandfather's best friend, whose daughter was my mother's bridesmaid. Mr. Kinzie had to abandon his house several times because of Indian depredations. The site of his old home is now fairly humming with industrial activities.

The boulevard I overlook is one of the busiest thoroughfares in the world. Thousands of cars pass every hour over the fine bridge which spans the river and gives access to two street levels. It is almost on the very spot where my grandmother used to pull herself across the river on a ferryboat drawn by a rope. On the north side of this river she used to pick blueberries, ready to fly any moment if she heard an Indian approaching.

Just beneath where I sit stood Fort Dearborn, the little fort with its wooden stockade which formed an outpost against Indians, and here, eighty-seven years ago, my mother was born, the third white girl born in Chicago.

The noise of the motors, the whistling of the tugs on the river, the traffic policeman's warning, the roar of the crowd, penetrate to my office, and I marvel at the great changes which have been wrought within three generations and even in my own life time.

Chicago—the little outpost in the wilderness

where deer drank from the river, wolves howled at night, and Indians lurked in the shadows.

Chicago—peopled by indomitable early settlers with energy, courage and perseverance, and, above all, with vision. They saw the great advantages of a situation at the foot of the Great Lakes, surrounded by the fertile corn and wheat fields of the West, and they laid the foundation of what is soon to be, not only one of the largest, but one of the most beautiful cities in the world.

The University of Illinois Press
is a founding member of the
Association of American University Presses.

University of Illinois Press
1325 South Oak Street
Champaign, IL 61820–6903
www.press.uillinois.edu